CHRIST IS LORD

MOSCOW, IDAHO

Mere
Christendom

Mere Christendom

Douglas Wilson

 CANON PRESS

MOSCOW, IDAHO

Library of Congress Cataloging-in-Publication Data:
Wilson, Douglas, 1953- author.
Mere Christendom / Douglas Wilson.
Moscow, Idaho : Canon Press, [2023] | Includes bibliographical
   references.
LCCN 2023005185 | ISBN 9781957905570 (paperback)
LCSH: Secularism. | Christianity and politics. | Church and
   state.
Classification: LCC BL2747.8 .W47 2023 | DDC 211/.6—dc23/
eng/20230301
LC record available at https://lccn.loc.gov/2023005185

23 24 25 26 27 28 29 30   10 9 8 7 6 5 4 3 2 1

For Knox

Contents

Part Three: Lies about Mere Christendom

Part Four: How to Restore Christendom

Preface

I n the waning days of the British Empire, one wit complained that "everything was at sea, except for the fleet." We think we can relate to this, except that as Americans, who like to think that because we do everything bigger, faster, and on a grander scale, we think that *our* cultural disintegration has to be more in the grand style—kind of like a Super Bowl halftime gone wrong, as being watched by someone who had just dropped a couple of hits of contaminated acid. If the last few years are anything to go on, it certainly seems that way.

I am offering this book to evangelical Christians, and evangelical Christians are quite accustomed to the basic thesis of this book, which is that "Jesus is the answer." But because they are also accustomed to express this sentiment in ways that artfully dodge the real issues, we should perhaps take just a moment to look at things more closely.

Jesus is the answer, but to which questions? The way we usually frame it, we mean that He is the answer to the problems of personal guilt and need, and then personal salvation after that.

The point of this book is that Jesus is the answer to every ultimate question that can be framed by man, and that this is not limited to the first person singular—"Why am I here? Where am I going? Why am I so guilty? Is there a way out? How should I then live along the way? Who am I accountable to?" These are all wonderful questions, and they are the necessary starting point. Individuals as individuals must get right with God, and a man must be born again if he is to see the kingdom of God. Thus far our evangelical pattern.

But at some point, we have to move on to the first person plural. "Why are *we* here? Where are we going? Why are we so guilty?" and all the rest. Cultures and societies and generations need Christ also. The Lord Jesus Christ is not just the answer to our personal dilemma. He is the eternal Logos of God, and as such, He is the spoken Answer to every legitimate question that any given society might pose, or all of mankind for that matter. His Lordship applies to politics, culture, entertainment, media, and His answers to our rebellions and follies are just exactly what we need to hear.

But if we want deliverance, we must call upon Him. We must name Him. Everyone who calls on the name of the

Lord will be saved. The framework for doing this is what I am calling *mere Christendom*, and hence this book.

I argue here for a principled abandonment of the disastrous experiment of secularism, and for a corporate confession of the fact that Jesus rose from the dead, and all done in such a way as to preserve and protect our liberties. This no doubt raises questions, and hence this book.

But before we get into it, I also need to share a few things about the structure and format of the book, which means that I should explain how it came about. Over the years, as I have argued for a proper understanding of the common law, natural revelation, American history, theocracy, Protestant resistance theory, free speech, and whatnot, a number of these elements began to take shape as a coherent "project."

As I posted a number of articles to my blog on these various issues, I started to attach a tag to them, and that tag was *mere Christendom*. They all had something in common, which is that over time they all contributed to a sprawling and smoking slag heap of words. They may have been sparkling and effervescent words, but it was a slag heap of them nonetheless—somewhere north of 400,000 of them. What I did was to hire my grandson, Knox Merkle, to work through all that material and pull out and arrange sections that could be used in a book like this, a book of ordinary size, and that was somewhat episodic or snapshotty in nature. You may wonder what *that* is supposed to mean, but it should become apparent to you quickly enough—provided you go ahead and read it.

At any rate, this assigned task of assembly was very ably performed by Knox, and then after that I wrote over the top of the whole thing, taking out infelicities and putting new ones in.

This book is therefore dedicated to Knox. It really is wonderful to have your children and grandchildren engaged in the battle together with you. And when that battle is the cultural equivalent of Helm's Deep, it is a particular encouragement.

Douglas Wilson
Moscow, Idaho

PART ONE

Where We Are Now

CHAPTER 1

The Wickedness of Secularism

W hat is secularism? Aside from being the villain of this book? Secularism is the idea that it is possible for a society to function as a coherent unit without reference to God. It is the idea that a culture can operate on the basis of a metaphysical and religious agnosticism. It is the idea that we can understand what human rights are without knowing what a human being actually is.

There are often occasions for many to trot out that apocryphal Luther quote about preferring to be governed by a wise

Turk than a foolish Christian. Right, but what if you get a foolish Turk? Now what? But even though Luther didn't say it, I would agree with him if he had—I personally would much rather be governed by a pagan who acted like a Christian than a Christian who acted like a pagan. But what we always seem to get are pagans who act like pagans, and then, when we object to *that*, we are soundly refuted by a misunderstanding of something Luther never said. All I want is a wise Christian. Is that too much to ask? Apparently.

In a Darwinian society, the highest civic value has to be survival, and since we are talking about species, it has to be survival of the *group*. There is therefore no theoretical ground for our secularist rulers to value individual liberty. The true ground of individual liberty is the recognition that individuals will live forever, and in a way that the current regime will not.

In order for genuine liberty to be extended to non-Christians, it is essential that non-Christians not be allowed to define genuine liberty. The blind should not lead the blind, as someone once taught us, and it is astonishing that even some Christians have been maneuvered into thinking that blind leadership can have any hope of keeping us on the road and out of the ditch.

The public square cannot be neutral. If Jesus is Lord, then Caesar isn't. If Jesus is Lord, the liberties of those who don't believe in Him are far more secure than the liberties of everybody in the hands of a Caesar who answers to no one above him.

☩

The liberties of the individual are too precious to be left in the hands of a civic agnosticism. To not know why you are extending liberties to the citizenry is to not know why you would be doing anything bad if you took them all away.

In Christian societies, overreach *is* a possibility. The Scriptures teach that all men are sinners, and men will sin in Christian societies as well as in secular ones. But in secular societies, overreach is not a *possibility*, but rather a necessity, by definition. If there is no God above the state, then the state has become god—the point past which there is no appeal. If there is a God above the state, then hubris in high places will always be dealt with appropriately.

Where the Spirit of the Lord is, there is liberty. If the Spirit has been exiled, how can we still have what only He can give? How can we reject the Giver and keep the gift? Those who puff themselves up and say that they can do this thing need to remember—wisdom is *always* vindicated by her children.

☩

When we look at what is happening to the culture around us, and we recognize that so much of the destruction is avoidable,

and we consider also the fact that the people implementing
these suicidal policies are not idiots—and indeed exhibit an
intelligence of the highest order in other areas—the conclusion appears inescapable. Our problems are spiritual. They
are the sort of moral problems that have always afflicted—
pardon the use of an anachronism—sinners.

Sinners always want salvation. The damned don't want
salvation—that is what it means to be damned. But sinners
aren't there yet, and so they are always casting about in
search of a savior. Of course it has to be a flattering savior,
one who will whisper soothing words on the way to the
bad place. This is because sinners want to be damned, sort
of, eventually. At least they prefer approaching damnation
to the only alternative, which is a real Savior, that is to say,
Jesus. And their preference stays this way unless a real Savior intervenes.

This is not just true on the individual level—although it
certainly is true there. We are social beings, which means
that we go to Heaven in groups, and we go to Hell in clusters. Civilizations are what they are because we, within those
civilizations, think the same way about things. Among these
things we should include the topics of sin and salvation.

Put this another way. There is no way to preach the gospel
clearly to an American without also preaching what America needs. And if you are not preaching what America needs,
what you are declaring ain't gonna save nobody in particular.
Of course, considering the way many preachers declare the
gospel these days, that may be (secretly) the point.

✛

One of the basic decisions confronting the secularists is whether they give priority to secularism, which is a result, or to democracy, which is a method. Democracy might wind up with a government that is not secular in the slightest, and a secular dictator might insist on a secular state despite the majority of his citizens wanting it to be some other way. Secularism and democracy are not synonyms.

If they were foundationally democrats, secularists ought not to mind, after 500 years, if an overwhelmingly Christian populace voted in the blue laws again, where ordinary commerce ceased on the Lord's Day. But if they are foundationally secularist, it doesn't matter to them if that is what a society-at-large wants to do. They are still against it. But why?

Conservative Christians are suspicious of democracy also, so that is not my point. Being suspicious of the results that democracy might come up with is a perfectly respectable way to be—if there was one thing that gave some of the Founders bad sweats in the middle of the night, it would be democracy. H.L. Mencken once defined democracy as the establishment of truth by the expedient of counting noses, and promulgating the results afterward with a club. Democracy can do bad things, like federally subsidized entitlements for instance, and that is why we need a constitutional republic, where certain things are recognized as off the table. Certain basic issues are not up for a vote.

This is why it is important that we have certain inalienable rights that our *Creator* gave us, and not rights that were bequeathed by the latest referendum, or by the kindness of the king. If the Lord gives, only the Lord can take away. If the state gives, then the state can take away, and blessed be the name of the state.

The point here is that the Christian has a natural point of appeal above every human institution—whether that institution be popular elections, that fortress of fraud we call the Congress, the faux-imperial White House, or the black-robed Nazgul who ghoulishly prey on the unborn. One of them singly, or all of them together, can be withstood by one courageous man with an open Bible. "You may not, as Yahweh reigns, do this thing." To take such a stand would require courage, as John the Baptist had to have in order to rebuke Herod, but to take such a stand would not require an ability to follow a convoluted set of political contradictions. Life is simple. God outranks the king. The king is to do what God says, not the other way around. "What a strange religion you Christians have!" I can hear someone saying.

But for the secularist, what outranks the highest human authority? What text can a secularist point to when he is trying to stand against certain democratic measures? It matters not if the democratic measure is a great idea or a howler. So long as he differs with it, it should not matter to him if the people are voting to close Home Depot on Sundays, or if they are not suffering a witch to live. There is no God above the people, right? Imagine there's no Heaven; it's easy if you try.

�֍

The secular state dispenses freedoms (it would be better to call them *privileges*) like they were party favors. They function as bribes. They serve as . . . bread . . . or circuses. As Chesterton points out somewhere, sexual license is the first and most obvious bribe to be offered to a slave. For many in our era, that was the bribe that ushered them into their bondage to the state.

If we are to have rights at all, in the strong sense, they must come from God. God-given rights cannot be revoked by any agency of man. If such rights are not grounded in the will of God, then whatever space I might be allowed to move around in is something that can be revoked. The state gives, and the state takes away, and blessed be the name of the state.

This is why secular conservatism, and secular libertarianism are both impotent against the collectivist idol of the state. The state, by insisting on secularism, is making sure that there never arises a school of thought that maintains the state is a creature, accountable to God like all other creatures. For if *that* idea takes root, it becomes possible for the state to hear a rebuke from outside the system, which it absolutely does not want to hear. These people want every possible rebuker to receive a security clearance first—and they are the ones in charge of the security clearances. But that is not the kind of ambassador YHWH sends.

✖

Now if certain Christians start to think that the secular project is actually a five-gallon bucket of lamesauce, what then?
Well, any purveyor of such crazy talk will be immediately
dismissed by the secularists as a neo-Confederate ayatollah
weird beard, and the Christians who have made their peace
with this present world will join in the denunciations, so
that they might get back to their missional outreach work
with that rising Demas demographic.

The choice between secular options on the right is like a
competition between a gentlemanly Epicurean and a rowdy
one. The former walks at dawn in a manicured flower garden, contemplating chess moves and Rawlsian political theory, while the latter is more interested in crack cocaine and
hoochie mamas. Without an overarching standard governing the two of them, we are simply comparing a longer life
of nobler, milder pleasures, and a shorter life consisting of a
blowout filled with orgiastic ones. But when we have to choose
on those grounds, it is simply a matter of personal preference.

The secular conservative wants industry, thrift, and hard
work. Oh, and low taxes. The secular libertarian wants to
smoke pot and marry another guy. But neither of them have
any ultimate standard to which the overweening state must
submit. The power relation goes the other way. The state, for
its purposes, will encourage the latter fellow, for he is helping to perpetuate a society of disconnected and atomistic
individuals, who are much more manageable. The state will
also tend to tolerate the former, grudgingly, because he has a
job and an income, and is kind of a cash cow.

But introduce the lordship of Jesus Christ over every facet of life, and see how the whole equation changes. Liberty is no longer "what I, the automaton, please," but rather what Jesus says I should be allowed to do. Under the authority of Christ, not only should I be free but so should my neighbor be, in the same way and on the same terms. If he is doing something that Jesus said was okay for him to do, then why should I hassle him? Or fine him? Or make him fill out forms? Or walk through a nudie scanner?

This is only possible when the gospel of Jesus Christ has been proclaimed in power, and men have received it and have been brought into the fellowship of the Father through the blood of Jesus. When men have been set free in this sense, set free from their *sins*, then it makes sense to speak of free men creating free markets. It is not possible otherwise. Every other defense of "free" markets is equivocating on the use of the word *free*.

This is also why it is possible to say that Jesus hates socialism. He hates statism. He hates crony crapitalism. Why? Because it doesn't run on love. Love is obligatory, but it is not coercive. Coercion, masked as it is by the lies of modern statist theory, is their great counterfeit of love.

If a man has been set free by Christ, he has been set free to love others. He has not been set free in order to run through the vibe field of impersonal market forces, making random purchases. The free market (the real one) is not a deistic machine. Rather, it is people loving each other in accordance with the law of Christ.

So freedom is defined by Jesus Christ. He defines it both positively and negatively. He sets us free to do as we ought, which is to love one another. He also sets us free negatively, establishing the boundaries that enable others to respect and love me by respecting and loving those boundaries. In the same way, I am set free to love him by respecting what God has given to him. God has posted signs everywhere that say *meum* and *tuum*. So if you don't love the sexual laws of Scripture, and you don't love the property right set forth in Scripture, then it is very simple. You don't love your neighbor.

How do I love my neighbor? Let me count the ways. I do it by not coveting his stuff. I love him by not coveting his wife, or his house, or his manservant or his maidservant, or his riding lawn mower. I love him as his immediate neighbor, looking across the fence at him. I also must love him when looking across the table at him in a zoning commission hearing. The Bible does not say "thou shalt not steal, except by majority vote."

When done rightly, it is not done because his liberty or mine is being taken as an absolute. What kind of sense would that make? It is being done because his liberty, just as much as mine, is the grace of God. And what must we do with the grace of God? We must receive it, treasure it, hold it, and embrace it. We must die before we let it go.

And this is why all Christian discussion of economic theory must begin with a full-throated denial of secularism. We must begin with the Lordship of Jesus Christ. In this Christian context, within these constraints, we could have a productive debate between a theocratic libertarian, a theocratic conservative, and a theocratic classical liberal. It would be productive because we would have a common standard to appeal to.

In short, the price of admission to a true Christian debate on economics is the confession of the crown rights of King Jesus. Visualize world peace, which means visualizing the nations discipled. In that day, when the lion and the lamb lie down together, and the children are chasing the cobras, does anybody seriously think that we will still be mailing half our potable income to that bloated monstrosity on the Potomac? So that ten million federal employees might have something to drink and pee away?

Without such a standard, our debate will consist of us just waving tatters and remnants of systems that once were godly, and citing passages from books that nobody reads any more. And without that standard, at the end of our debate, we would all just look at the moderating state to find out what was legal. Not very much, the answer turns out.

In the meantime, those who defend free markets on the basis of biblical law (and their only possible basis in the gospel of free grace) cannot be said to be doing so because they have in any sense made freedom an absolute. Only the word of Christ is absolute.

Someone might reply that I am just bringing in "Jesus" to justify my love of the free market—doing so quite conveniently, but still after the fact nonetheless. How, the scoffing might continue, are we supposed to figure out what economic principles your "Jesus" might prefer? Ah, I would reply, we are extremely fortunate. He wrote a book on it.

One of the characteristics of lust is that it hates to be constrained. This applies as much to political lusts as to sexual desire, and it explains a great deal about the dishonesty of the progressive mentality. How many times, when you have asked someone a specific question about some important issue, have you been told by that person that he "hates labels." I dare say. Labels interfere with getting what you want. People remind you tomorrow of what you said yesterday, and this restricts your freedom of movement.

Augustine wrote wisely of the *libido dominandi*, the lust for power, characteristic of so many progs on the campaign trail, and even more characteristic of them when they get hold of the levers of power.

Those who are in favor of smaller government are, when this is translated, in favor of a smaller capacity for coercion. Those who are in favor of bigger government are in favor of increased opportunities for coercion. The *libido dominandi* is therefore characteristic of those who want more access to coercive policies, and it is not characteristic of those who don't want that. So if someone says, using labels, that he is pro-life, pro-free market, anti-big government, he is saying that he believes we must reject the temptations of *libido dominandi*, just as someone who says he is quitting smoking is saying, as a natural consequence, that he wants to stop buying cigarettes. But someone who has cartons of cigarettes stacked up in his basement has no intention of quitting. So suppose we saw those stacks of cartons and commented, "So you're a smoker, then?" and then we were told that he "really hates labels." What he really hates is being caught. He hates being called on what he is doing.

Now in passing, I should acknowledge that there are conservative types who don't hate labels, but who use them in the most clunkity fashion imaginable. I have personal experience with this; I speak as a close observer of some conservatives whose worldview is made out of cinder blocks and cheap cement. Okay, that happens. In the theological sphere, with confessions and creeds, and in the political sphere with platforms and campaign slogans, and so on, there are those who cannot handle some of the subtleties of the world God made. That is a problem, sure enough, but in our age, it is *not* a huge one. The intellectual life of our age is characterized by a squishy goulash of subtleties all the way to the bottom of the

pot, a farrago of pomothot, and the purveyors of this pomothot are often quite clever—they don't hate labels because
they can't follow arguments. They hate labels because they
can follow them, and those arguments get in the way of their
lusts. Remember that the devil is a dialectician.

✴

If relativism is the case (and secularism is a form of relativism), then anything goes. If relativism is the case, then anything goes, *including the worst forms of absolutism.* This is why,
incidentally, secularism has mounted such a pitiful response
to the demands of fundamentalist Islam.

Secularism is relativistic, of necessity, because all societies
reflect the nature and attributes of their god. If man is god,
as he is in secularism, then the ethics of that society will
reflect the nature of man. But man changes all the time. He
is unstable, like water. Secular ethics is relativistic because
man, the god of the system, is himself relative. He is relative
to his genetics, his environment, his upbringing, and he says
whatever comes into his head. And whatever comes into his
head becomes law. For the time being.

✴

The response of secularism to radical Islam makes no sense,
at least on paper. Why worry about hypothetical fundamentalist Christians who *might* execute a blasphemer centuries

from now, and in the name of resisting this threat make common cause with radical Muslims who are executing blasphemers this very minute? Some might say we *do* stand up to them—don't we bomb them? No, we bomb some of them and cozy up to others. Many of those we cozy up to are the worst. But we shouldn't spend too much time trying to make sense of it, because it doesn't make sense. If it made sense, it wouldn't be sin.

Where this does make *some* sense is in the fact that the root of secularism is actually a rejection of the Christian faith, and the root of Islam is also a rejection of the Christian faith. Anything but Christianity, and anyone but Jesus. This is the commonality that trumps everything else. This is the hidden tie that binds.

☧

Here are the markers of the god of the system:

First, the god of the system is the final court of appeal. There is no appeal beyond him. Once you get to his court, and the decision has been made, the matter is settled. If you continue to resist after that point, then you are a disruptive rebel and an enemy of mankind. You are out of the appeals process and into the justice system.

Second, the god of the system requires that his words be interpreted according to the historical/grammatical hermeneutic. Lots of legal theorists think that the Constitution is a living document, which is elastic and stretchy, but only when you are stretching it to the left. The fact that you can mess around with constitutional words in this creative way means that the words of the Constitution are *not* part of the god of the system. But notice how nobody ever says that the majority opinions in pursuit of judicial activism are "living documents" also. No, you have to interpret *their* words with sobriety and respect, no funny business, and why? Where respect for the plain meaning of words is demanded, you have identified the god of the system.

And last, the god of the system is the fountainhead of morality. This is why Christians have an easy distinction in their minds between "legal" and "moral." But for those who believe that there is no intelligence beyond our corporate and collective intelligence, there can ultimately be no such distinction. Right? Christians worship the God who is outside all our systems—He is transcendent—and that is why we can distinguish sins and crimes.

☧

Godless secularism still maintains an impressive facade. Like an ornate shell of a long dead creature of the deep blue sea, there is enough to keep quite a number of people from pointing out the obvious, to wit, that the shell is hollow.

So a lot of people have conspired together to not notice what is going on. The reasons for this conspiracy can be summed up in one word, which is *paycheck*. But there are reasons for believing this cannot be kept up for much longer.

The strength still manifested by the West is all residual or borrowed. The residual is left over from previous generations when men were more faithful, and the shell, while hollow, still has some strength. The borrowed is taken from the red state enclaves. That game cannot be kept up much longer.

CHAPTER 2

Taxation

A story is told of a fellow who was mugged in an alley by a band of thugs, and he put up a ferocious fight. After about fifteen minutes, they got him down on the ground and found just two dollars in his wallet. "Two dollars?" one of them said. "You put up that fight for two dollars?"

"Well, no, actually. I thought you were after the $500 in my boot."

One of the most precious possessions a government has is its moral legitimacy. When they have it, taxes are paid, for the most part, voluntarily. Any society requires force for the outliers but is not held together at the center by force. When the ruling elites start to opt out of this societal bond—"laws are for the little people"—there is usually a time lag, but the "little people" do catch on. And when they catch on, the whole thing spirals down into chaos.

One of the central techniques that is used by despots for divesting themselves of moral legitimacy is the technique of governing through arbitrary administrative law. A free people live under laws passed by legislatures in which they have freely chosen representatives. The prerogative of passing such laws may not be transferred. So if you chafe under rules and regs that spew forth from all the alphabet agencies, then you are not free. It doesn't matter that you are currently not being harassed. No despot can torment all his slaves simultaneously.

When there is no standard above the state, then the state becomes the standard. If there is no God above the system, then the system becomes god. And because the state is always ravenous for tax money, the tax burden gradually becomes a monstrosity. The people carrying this burden have gotten gradually used to it and don't even notice anymore how radically unscriptural it all is.

We are currently living under a form of government that our Constitution was explicitly designed to prevent. We are told *ad nauseam* that we are a free people, while at the same time our administrative managers, our ruling elites, reserve to themselves the right to dictate to us pretty much anything that comes into their heads. They walk the corridors of power with the demeanor you might expect from such little gods.

Obviously it is a sin to steal, and it is not a sin to be stolen from. The first part is flat prohibited in Scripture (Exod. 20:15; Eph. 4:28), and the second part is intuitively obvious. Better to be wronged than to do wrong. But when making this point that it is not a sin to be stolen from, we are talking about someone sneaking into your garage at two in the morning and taking your bicycle. It is not wrong to be wronged in this way.

Our current sin is found in the *way* we are being stolen from. When God prohibits stealing, this assumes the institution of private property. When God prohibits adultery, what is in the background? Unless there is such a thing as marriage, you cannot have adultery. Adultery is defined as violation of marriage vows. In the same manner, stealing is a violation of someone's right to remain in possession of their own property.

So the requirement here is to learn a little blunt force honesty with yourself. It is not a sin to write a big check to the government. It is not a sin to be stolen from. It is a sin to write that check and tell yourself that you are just "doing your share." That is the sin of being delusional when God has required us to be clear-headed. It is a sin to believe that our government is anything other than a pirate ship of the thieves, by the thieves, and for the thieves. It is a sin to go on believing the lies when we have no good reason to.

In short, the first step for the Christian taxpayer is the same as what you find in addiction recovery groups. First you have to admit you have a problem.

I am required to love all men because all men bear the image of God, and it is not possible to love a man without simultaneously respecting his stuff.

"For this, Thou shalt not commit adultery, Thou shalt not kill, *Thou shalt not steal,* Thou shalt not bear false witness, *Thou shalt not covet*; and if there be any other commandment, it is briefly comprehended in this saying, namely, Thou shalt love thy neighbour as thyself" (Rom. 13:9, emphasis added).

There are two moral imperatives here that presuppose private property—the prohibition of stealing and the prohibition of coveting. None of these prohibitions should be over-engineered. I cannot commit adultery if there is no marriage. I cannot murder if there is no right to life. I cannot bear false witness if there is no truth. And, bringing this to the point, I cannot steal or covet unless there is such a thing as my neighbor having a right to whatever is modified by his very own personal pronoun. To adapt the nouns from the tenth commandment—his house, his servants, his livestock, or anything else that is HIS.

This requirement to love extends from the lowest strata of society to the very top. Paul tells those who make their living as thieves to steal no longer, but to get an honest job, working with their hands. But what about the "high and lonely destiny" that the lords of the earth would like to have? Sure, the Bible prohibits pickpockets, but where do I get the authority to relegate the mighty ones who pass our tax laws (in their august and solemn assemblies) to the status of those who say *arrrgh*, and who have a parrot on their shoulders?

Well, it's like this. More Bible thumping. When Samuel warns the people against anointing a king like the other nations have, he warns them of the consequences to their property. In other words, it is reasonable to worry about the pickpockets in town, but wise men worry about another set of men, whose grasp of the distinction between *meum* and *tuum* is every bit as tenuous. These rulers will rise to the pinnacles of hubris, claiming to be equal to God, deserving of a tenth.

> And he will take your fields, and your vineyards, and your oliveyards, even the best of them, and give them to his servants. And he will take the tenth of your seed, and of your vineyards, and give to his officers, and to his servants. And he will take your menservants, and your maidservants, and your goodliest young men, and your asses, and put them to his work. He will take the tenth of your sheep: and ye shall be his servants. And ye shall cry out in that day because of your king which ye shall have chosen you; and the LORD will not hear you in that day. (1 Sam. 8:14–18)

If we got *back* to a ten percent taxation rate, we would think we were living in a libertarian's daydream. We are pretty far gone. We have forgotten that liberty must be understood in terms of durable goods.

Last example, showing that the requirement to love a man by respecting his stuff is not limited to street urchins. Kings are included. Kings are singled out, actually. Let's talk about Naboth's vineyard, shall we?

Ahab the king broke the tenth commandment and coveted Naboth's property. He had a case of the sulks about it, until his wife suggested that he institute land reform, or zoning regulations, or inheritance taxes, or targeting the one percent. Something like that. The greedmeisters call their "reforms" by many different names, but greasy envy is always in the mix. You can read all about it in 1 Kings 21:1–29.

This is why a bedrock qualification for political office is that a man must fear God, love the truth, *and hate covetousness* (Exod. 18:21). Do we have that in the halls of Congress? Not even a little bit close.

Because taxes can be a form of theft, and because taxes need not be theft at all, a reasonable question to ask is how we can tell the difference.

The baseline, the starting point, is that property belongs to the individual. He is the one that *Thou shalt not steal* applies to. He is the one with the house, the vineyard, the lawn mower, the wallet, the smartphone, and so on. Whenever the Bible talks about property, it always talks about it in two categories. The first is God's absolute ownership of all things (Deut. 10:14), and the second is the relative ownership that you and your neighbor enjoy (Deut. 8:18). When we talk about the state possessing things, this possession is derivative. The state extracts value from the taxpayer, the appointed steward of God's wealth, and this extraction can also be divided into two categories. This value can be extracted lawfully, or the state can play the role of the thief. So how are we to tell the difference?

We know that taxation can be done right because the Bible talks about paying taxes to the one to whom it is due (Rom. 13:7). These are taxes that we *owe*, and they may not be considered theft at all. We should no more chafe at paying our legitimate taxes than we do paying our bill for satellite television. There are taxes we do not owe, but ought to pay anyway, having more important things to do. This is the meaning of what Jesus teaches Peter—we don't owe it, but go ahead and pay it (Matt. 17:24–27).

And then there are other circumstances where the illegitimate taxes have become so onerous, and the justification for them so outlandish, and tax courts have beclowned themselves to such an extent, that the Lord raises up a left-handed means for the children of Israel to pay their tribute (Judg. 3:15–19).

Now I am not issuing any kind of call to action, other than the action of understanding what the heck occurreth.

It is long past time for us to be sons of Issachar, understanding the times and knowing what Israel should do (1 Chron. 12:32). In our circumstance, deliverance would be ours if most of us came to the *simple recognition* that our ruling elites are governing unlawfully. They are illegitimate.

So this brings us back to the earlier question. How do we tell what kind of taxation is challenging the law of God as opposed to the taxation that is in line with the law of God? There are three basic criteria.

First, the level of taxation must not rival God (1 Sam. 8:15). God claims a tithe, and if that is all God needs, and if God is a jealous God, then we ought to see any attempt on the part of the civil government to go past ten percent as an aspiration to Deity. This is the perennial temptation for fallen man (Gen. 3:5), particularly for rulers of all kinds (Isa. 14:13), and so that temptation must not be funded. Cutting off the government at nine percent is like refusing a third Scotch to a wobbly tavern-goer at 1:00 a.m. Shouldn't be controversial.

Second, the taxes need to be levied, in the main, so that the rulers can perform the functions that God requires them to perform. Coercion is a big deal, and so the government must only be allowed to exercise it when they have express warrant from the Scriptures for what they are doing. If they have express warrant to hunt down murderers, and they do, then they have express warrant to collect money to pay for certain men to do this. They are God's deacon of justice, and the deacon of justice needs to be paid just like the rest of us (Rom. 13:4). They are not allowed to collect fees to pay for activities that are prohibited to them. If they are not allowed to do it in the first place, they are not allowed to tax us to pay for it. To do so would be theft.

Third, the taxes must be lawful and in accordance with the established constitution of the people. Arbitrary and capricious government, when the constitution outlaws arbitrary and capricious government, is hypocritical. It sits in judgment upon us in points of law, and contrary to the law it commands us to be struck. Since I have no particular person in mind, I may feel free to echo Paul's sentiment about this without overstepping any personal boundaries—the men who do this are a whited wall (Acts 23:3).

So then, in summary, taxes are theft when the government is aspiring to be god in the lives of its subjects, when the government is refusing to do what the real God requires of them and is doing something else instead, usually something very expensive, and when the government is not obeying its own legitimate processes for levying taxes.

When you get lots of pirate ships, what do you have? This is not a trick question. You have a pirate fleet. You have lots of pirates. Augustine records a time when a pirate was captured and brought before Alexander the Great. The pirate asked why he was styled a pirate for doing to ships what Alexander was doing to countries, and, despite this, Alexander was styled a great emperor.

History is silent as to what became of the witty pirate then, but his question did have a certain resonance. Secular man, with covetous loins, hands, and brains, has not yet been able to answer it. There is, however, a stiff fine for raising the question in inappropriate ways.

I am not issuing a call to action, but rather a call for understanding and *recognition*. Clearly this is not because action is irrelevant, but rather because rash and precipitous action is usually destructive. Think, and *then* do. At some point, action will be necessary, and when that day comes, Christians need to have consciences that are prepared for the necessary action. If you are going to run a marathon, you don't get ready for it by running around the block the day before.

Laws multiply when the lawgivers want to have subjects instead of citizens. When laws swarm like the frogs of Egypt, the reason for it is to increase guilt. This guilt means two things—one is that when there are multitudinous regulations, they can always get you for something. Second, it turns everyone into a lawbreaker, but because our consciences are not trained by the Scriptures, when it gets to the point of resistance, we are dragged into the fray with uneasy consciences—instead of walking toward the confrontation with a clean heart and well-oiled shield.

Swarms of their froggy little laws, and swarms of officers to eat out our substance, are a threat to us. What is a threat to them? Well, the gospel is the enemy of tyrants everywhere precisely because the gospel liberates the conscience. Even if for years after conversion, every forgiven sinner does nothing explicitly political against the tyrants, the tyrant nevertheless objects to the fact that the gospel is plainly removing all his handles from the sinners. A forgiven man is a free man, a fact regarded by taskmasters everywhere with frank suspicion.

If you doubt what I say about how these laws are a teeming nuisance, utterly inconsistent with living as free men and women, this is just because you don't want to come to grips with the fact that you are probably committing a felony right this minute. Have you ever thrown away some junk mail that came to your house addressed to somebody else? That, my friend, is punishable by a sentence of up to five years. Now if you receive this information, and then next week you receive a missive about a sale at Macy's addressed to Harry Schwartz, and you are not he, and you blithely throw it in the regular garbage (instead of the mandatory recycle bin, you villain!), and you do all this without any qualms of conscience whatever, it means that you are actually making some real progress. We might make a Christian of you yet.

Now some like to respond to this emphasis on *property rights as human rights* as a thinly veiled defense of "it's mine, I tell you!" I make the mistake of issuing a clarion call for integrity as we learn how to stand up to the gargantuan thievery of the modern state, and defenders of that kleptocracy can only hear me saying, "We wants it, we needs it. Must have the precious. They stole it from us. Sneaky little Hobbitses."

☧

This is all part of what I mean by beginning with "recognition." The early Christians trusted in God, which is why they could joyfully accept it when their property was plundered. When the prehensile and rapacious state seizes my property, like a dragon from the north, I should accept it from the hand of God—with the same principled contentment I ought to display if I lost my earthly goods in an earthquake or fire. It's only stuff.

> For you had compassion on those in prison, and you joyfully accepted the plundering of your property, since you knew that you yourselves had a better possession and an abiding one. (Heb. 10:34, ESV)

In other words, I don't object to them stealing my stuff because I am revealed as a heart idolater by *their* attempts at stealing (Eph. 5:5). If God's object is to reveal my undue attachment to stuff, He could do that by means of fire, flood, high winds, or congressmen saving the children. And if a property owner's idolatry is revealed by whatever circumstance, then it stands revealed. But whether or not the victim was an idolater, the thief who revealed that idolatry to the world remains a thief.

When Job lost all his worldly goods, some of it was because of natural disaster (Job 1:19) and some of it was by human agency (Job 1:27). But Job attributed all of it to God and submitted to God's will in it. The fact that he recognized the hand of the Lord in all of it, and accepted that loss from the Lord, did not mean that he had acquiesced to a new economic theory as developed by Chaldean raiding parties, or socialists, but I repeat myself.

So before we charge off to save our goods, we need to learn that they are in fact being stolen, and we need to get this information down into our wee little brains. After that information has simmered there for a number of years, and we start to notice a certain lightness of step, and a certain spring in our conscience, then we might be equipped to formulate a plan of action that was not certifiably insane.

So we accept the plundering of our goods joyfully, while naming it as plunder. Naming the plunder is the first step in learning eventually how to put a stop to it. For the magistrate to take property from anyone without scriptural warrant is theft *simpliciter*. The fact that we are used to it justifies nothing. Illicit taxation is theft, just as the fabled *droit du seigneur* was sexual immorality—whether or not all parties cooperated.

Being a creature, I reason from axioms and decline the invitation to prove my axioms. A good axiom should therefore occupy a place on the trunk down near the grass, and not be a set of twigs up near the airy heavens, and so here it is.

We are created by God, and it is self-evident that we were endowed by that Creator with certain rights that are inalienable, and that among these rights are the right to life, liberty, and property. If someone claims that I am refusing to pick up the *onus probandi*, the burden of proof, I will simply laugh contentedly and acknowledge that this is entirely correct. I believe the burden of proof should actually be on the guy with a gun who wants to rob me. He is not hard to identify—he usually has big block letters on the back of his jacket. Ask *him* what he is doing.

Being a magistrate is not a universal "it's all okay" permission slip. Taxation without representation is theft. Taxation to finance cockamamie wars is theft. Taxation to pay wheat farmers to not grow wheat is theft. Taxation to fund Planned Parenthood is murderous theft. Taxation to fund research programs into whether cocaine causes quail to engage in risky sexual behavior is theft. Taxation to buy fuel for the 100,000 backhoes dumping our money into the Fannie Mae sinkhole is theft.

And not being able to see theft in all this is tantamount to standing on the top of the levee in the middle of Hurricane Katrina and being unable to "detect the breeze," and asking the rescue worker pulling on your elbow to please "define breeze."

CHAPTER 3

Tactics of the Enemy

O ne of the central tactics of our regnant secularism is to pretend that their foundational assumptions are religiously neutral, and that we need not look at them. In other words, they hide the foundation they have poured, they hide the blueprints of the building they want to build, and if you point to that foundation, or to the blueprints they are holding behind their back, they resort to calling you a conspiracy theorist. A time will come when they are open about it, but until then, they deny that their atheistic secularism leads of necessity to moral anarchy. But it has to.

When I was in high school, I took a sociology class, and it was just the kind of class you might expect. One day the teacher came in (a very nice young lady) and asked if any of us had ever been afraid of a black person. I helpfully raised my hand, and she called on me, pleased at this opportunity for us to do some helpful relating. "And why do you think you were afraid of him?" she asked, wanting to get to the root of some of our societal problems. "Because he had a knife," I said.

Now to be perfectly fair, we were kids, and it wasn't much of a knife. But it was enough of a knife to scare me at the time, and to make me seek help years later in my sociology class.

This was the same teacher who, on another occasion, taught us all that all teenagers went through a time when they hated their parents. But I didn't, and I raised my hand and honored my parents by saying that I loved them. She said, no, that wasn't true.

Words form societal expectation; words catechize; words build. And if there is another civilization in the way, words tear down. In *The Abolition of Man*, Lewis provides a striking quote from an old English song about Herod—"and so he sent the word to slay, and slew the little childer."[1]

So let's return to the question of "fearing" whoever it is now. There is a missing premise in the question, which is that all such fear is irrational, a point that is reinforced by the increasingly fashionable use of the suffix *–phobia*. Some unfortunate people won't go outside anymore because of a

---

1. C.S. Lewis, *The Abolition of Man* (1944; New York: HarperCollins, 1974), 1.

phobia about a bee getting in their hair. Others are irrationally afraid of enclosed spaces, and others have hyper-jitters about heights.

So there are irrational fears, for which the suffix *–phobia* works quite well, and then there is the PC-point that is advanced with every use of that suffix in words like *homophobia* or *Islamophobia*.

You should see the tactic clearly—any opposition to their agenda, for whatever reason, is dismissed as a mental illness. It was the Soviet Union that first pioneered this tactic, because anyone who opposed the establishment of that glorious paradise was obviously sick in the head. You obviously need treatment. They haul you away to their reeducation centers more in pity than in anger.

Christians therefore have no business using such words, unless it is to make fun of them. I know lots of Christians who think that Leviticus and Romans exclude homosexual behavior, but I don't know any Christians who have an irrational fear of homosexuals. I know many Christians who don't believe that Mohammad was Allah's prophet, but I don't know any who have an irrational fear of Muslims. And when prudence dictates extra precautions, what some might call *fearful* precautions—say you are flying to an airport that is on the State Department's list of dumb places to fly to— that is hardly an irrational fear. One soldier does not turn to another, right before they go over the top, and ask if he ever struggles with bulletphobia. "Why, yes," the reply might come. "Thanks for this opportunity to open up a bit. I think

my mother must not have tucked me in enough at night
when I was little."

Words matter. The word *phobia* is a weapon. So are words
like Christendom—used negatively or positively—and
words like community and missional.

Chesterton says somewhere that the modern world has
insisted on exiling the Savior, but has done so from the
midst of the story of the Gadarene demoniac. The upshot
of this means that our naked public square has been purged
of any reference to Jesus, but we are now left with the devils
and with the swine.

Too many times Christians have placed the consequences
of not believing in Jesus too far off in the eschatological distance. The things we say about that placement are quite true,
as far as it goes—to be admitted into the presence of God we
must be clothed in the righteousness of Jesus Christ, and if
we are banished from the presence of God on that great day,
it will be because we never knew Him.

But not knowing Him does not just result in Hell later. It
also means that when we refuse to acknowledge Him here
and now, the end result is that we start building little proto-
types of Hell in order to test-drive them. And that is why the
public square rapidly becomes a haunt for owls and jackals.

Another thing to keep in mind is that the devils know
how to work us in two ways. Too many conservative

Christians tend to think that the devil simply wants to tempt us with variations on the orgy porgy debauch. But the devil is actually parsimonious—he hates pleasure and only uses it to bait the hook. If he can get us to take the naked hook, so much the better. The Gadarene demoniac was not living in luxury, remember, and the legion of demons was not feeding him grapes. Never forget that the devil at heart is a prohibitionist.

> Now the Spirit speaketh expressly, that in the latter times some shall depart from the faith, giving heed to seducing spirits, and doctrines of devils; Speaking lies in hypocrisy; having their conscience seared with a hot iron; Forbidding to marry, and commanding to abstain from meats, which God hath created to be received with thanksgiving of them which believe and know the truth. For every creature of God is good, and nothing to be refused, if it be received with thanksgiving: For it is sanctified by the word of God and prayer. (1 Tim. 4:1–5)

Doctrines of devils? Sounds interesting. What might *they* teach? Well, the devils want you to have sex issues along with a bunch of food issues, and that pretty much describes our generation down to a T. And many professing Christians—who are too embarrassed to name Jesus in the public square—are not too embarrassed to stampede along with all the food phobias that are dictated to us, not to mention being slowly affected by the gay pride parades that gyrate slowly past, and they do not put these two realities together. As Dylan taught us, you gotta serve somebody. It might be the devil, or it might be the Lord, but neutrality is no option at all.

Chesterton hammered those pinched souls who were well on their way to banning salt and pepper, along with mustard, as a most "unnatural stimulant." Those pinched souls don't know that they are pinched, and they don't know that they have been outmaneuvered, and that the only alternative to the path they are on is a good confession of the crown rights of Jesus Christ.

If Jesus is Lord, then this means that our lower intestine has been dethroned from its place of privilege and power. If the Lordship of Jesus is denied, then the only alternative, since our god is now our belly (Phil. 3:19), will be to confess the crown rights of the lower reaches of that belly, and to begin to leave bizarre and unnatural offerings on that altar.

Those offerings might include the sexual organ of another, or it might be fecal transplants. Whatever.

Regardless, the solution is to turn back to Jesus—not simply in our hearts, although it must begin there, but to do so on the steps of the county courthouse. When it comes down to it, there is fundamentally a basic choice. Either we will have a nativity set there, with Joseph, Mary, the baby Jesus, two cows, a goat, and a drummer boy, or we will have two (or more) homosexuals holding up their marriage license for the photographers.

✳

Not being an anarchist, I believe that some forms of coercion are good and necessary, but because I also believe that cops, legislators, judges, and SWAT teams are made up of sinners, it is absolutely necessary for us to know that we have warrant from the Almighty God before we try to make anybody do anything. Before fining someone, or flogging him, or putting him in jail, or exiling him, or executing him, which pretty much exhausts the options, we had better know that what we are doing is authorized by God. If it is, well and good. If it is not, then we are abusing someone created in the image of God, and God is going to hold us accountable for it. We should either coerce with a clean conscience (and an open Bible) or not at all.

Liberals do not like this form of argument, because they want to pretend that there is nothing whatever coercive about what they are doing. They are not taxing certain individuals at abusive rates while simultaneously threatening the inadequately cooperative with imprisonment. No, what they are actually doing is "asking" the "wealthy" to pay their "fair share." Oh, since you put it that way . . .

Look, if you don't do what they say, at some point in the proceedings, men with guns are going to show up at your house. I do not have a problem with this if those men with guns are going after a pedophile, or a rapist, or a murderer. Go ahead. Coerce away. If you need them, I will provide you with the verses that show that God approves of this kind of coercion. But if they are showing up at a man's house because he got tired of having bureaucrats pee a bunch of his money into the Potomac, then something has gone wrong somewhere. As the saying goes, the liberal idea of democracy is three coyotes and a sheep voting on what to have for lunch.

They don't want any limiting principle, in principle. *Thus far, and no farther*, is not a phrase that they like to find in the mouths of the voting public. It reminds them too much of that flag with the rattlesnake on it.

But in order to have a genuine limiting principle, one that works, it has to be grounded in the work and words of the God who made us all. One nation, under *God*. If God is not in the picture, then something or someone else will rise to the position of ultimate authority. If there is no God above Caesar, then how do we keep Caesar from declaring himself god? Not only so, but because as god he answers to no one, this means there is no such thing as ethics. There is no authority over him to which he must defer. And if that is the case, then everybody under him must defer to him—and he could well be an erratic or ill-tempered or insane god with bad digestion. And does anybody really want a god with a bad temper who is capable of getting toothaches or migraines?

So it is not surprising that they abuse language to hide the coercive nature of their project. And one of their signature moves is to turn the tables on anyone who identifies and objects to their coercions. It is "coercive" to identify what they are doing. It hurts their feelings. Well, tough.

☧

I am going to appeal to Girard here, but I need to say at the outset that Girard tries to throw all his valuable insights away by refusing to embrace the propitiatory nature of Christ's sacrifice. But even though he tries to throw those insights away, I will not do so.

One of the things that Girard noticed about the Scriptures, not to mention human history, is that oppression is always respectable, and that the victim who protests that oppression is not respectable. He is told to shut up. Persecutors always feel persecuted. The oppressor feels oppressed and is highly indignant when the victim won't shut up. When the victim writes a psalm of lament, he is not playing the dutiful role that he was assigned. The victim is therefore the troublemaker and must be dealt with.

One time Jesus told His interlocutors that they were trying to kill Him. They said He was nuts: "Did not Moses give you the law, and yet none of you keepeth the law? Why go ye about to kill me? The people answered and said, Thou hast a devil: who goeth about to kill thee?" (John 7:19–20).

Jesus knew the play that was being run on Him, and the people running the play did not know.

It is the same kind of thing here. Liberals want to stay respectable. This is why their threats are couched in the interrogative. Let's "ask" everybody to do this and haul them off if they don't. They want to draw a veil over their bloody and violent ways. If anyone pulls the veil back, then *he* is the troublemaker. Such a man is—to borrow the words of Ahab—a troubler of Israel (1 Kings 18:17).

Wanting to leave people to their lawful pursuits is not coercive. And neither is it coercive to identify those who will not—for love or money—leave them alone.

One of our difficulties is that conservatives confound the rule of law, which we want to fight for, with the orderliness of process, which is often used to distort and overturn the very meaning of righteousness. Many times we are outmaneuvered because we think we have an obligation to play by their rules all the time, even though their rules are ungodly. Believers should care about *righteousness* and let the bureaucrats care about their processes. Remember that, right after having committed the crime of all crimes, the murder of the Christ, when Judas came back and returned the thirty pieces of silver, these orderly process-mongers were very concerned about what account they put the money into. They didn't want to get dinged in the next audit. Ethics are so important.

Private persons should not be coerced into approval of what they know to be sin—that is where liberty of conscience applies. Assuming that something can be sinful without being criminal, a free citizen should have the right to disassociate himself from it, to not approve of it. But the public magistrate does not have liberty of conscience in this same way. The magistrate is God's *deacon*, God's *servant*, and is solemnly *charged by God* to reward the righteous and punish the wrongdoer (Rom. 13:1–4). This cannot be confounded with rewarding the wicked and punishing the righteous. That would be to frame mischief with a law (Ps. 94:20). And when the foundations are destroyed, what can the righteous do (Ps. 11:3)?

In *A Man for All Seasons*, Thomas More is portrayed as saying that you should not waive the law in order to get at the devil, for when you have done so, you find that you have no way to stand when he turns on you. More is talking about the importance of the rule of law, even when you desire to prosecute the devil. How do you prosecute the devil, in other words, without turning into the devil?

But this is quite different than standing by silently as you give the devil leave to write the laws, and to amend the laws as he pleases. I am with More if we are talking about honoring man-made laws, even if the defendant is the devil himself. But suppose the devil is the prosecutor. Now what?

Thomas More was talking about men who wanted to dispense with the rules of justice in order to achieve their idea of a "higher justice." If the culprit is *known* by us to be guilty, then why bother with trials and evidence? Why bother with hearing from both sides? We already are convinced in our own minds of the answer, and so let us proceed directly to the sentencing. This is the demented logic of lynch mobs, a subject I flatter myself as knowing something about.

There I was, I will tell my great-grandchildren, sitting on a skittish horse, hands behind my back, rope around my neck, and a learned academic voice called out from the crowd, "Ya! What does someone like *you* know about Girard?"

If there is one thing that Christians need to learn more about in this "click to convict" era, it is the importance of due process, presumption of innocence, hearing both sides argued, and so on.

And, with More, I would want to follow all these principles though the indicted man were the devil himself. But if the devil is the prosecutor, and has swathed himself in a multitude of wicked laws, you can be assured that none of them will protect anyone's rights. The devil is an accuser, and he detests anything that might slow his accusations down.

So what I outlined above—presumption of innocence, due process, and others like them, like the right to face your accuser—are what More would call man-made laws. But they are man-made methods for implementing biblical principles. They are instituted in a fallen world, which means that they might have the result of allowing a very guilty person to get off. But better that, More argues, than to insist on hanging a guilty man, but at the expense of mowing down all the laws that protect a hundred innocent men.

So we must never mow down the law to get at the devil. But not everything that is called a law is in fact a law in this older sense. Depending on the state, our current "law" allows for the dismemberment of little children, and that by the million. Our law *does* prohibit selling the pieces of these children, requiring instead that the children be thrown in a dumpster. Let us call it a dignity dumpster. That kind of law is *protecting no one.* That kind of law is what sixty million of our people needed protection *from.* Moreover, when the law prohibiting the sale of baby parts is openly violated, our lawless rulers not only refused to prosecute, they openly refused to cease subsidizing the practice. So our laws on this subject are not laws that, if removed, would allow the devil to turn on us. These laws *are* the devil turning on us.

And the laws of matrimony are not currently being upheld by our rulers, and merely extended to people who happen to be a little more creative with their sex organs. No, the goal is the abolition of marriage. These laws are not mildly adjusted marriage laws. They are laws that will have the effect, in the very near future, of nullifying and/or outlawing marriage. These current laws are not standing between us and the devil. These laws are the devil.

So then, in answer to an inaccurate application of More's principles to the resistance of lesser magistrates, we are not trying to mow down the law to get at the devil. The devil is mowing down the laws of many centuries in order to get at us.

And still the majority of Christians believe that they have a duty to stand by and watch it happen.

CHAPTER 4

Jesus Mobs

A number of you have been languishing out there for a while, listening to sermons from a man who, if he had been a character in *The Pilgrim's Progress*, would have been the Rev. Rabbitheart. But for the incoming troublous times, you need something a little more bracing than that. You might be in the position of an ancient Persian who surmised that the king and Haman were playing drinking challenge games again: "And the king and Haman sat down to drink; but the city Shushan was perplexed" (Esther 3:15).

Given that America is filling up with competing mobs now, one of the things that believing Christians ought to do is go back to the Scriptures to see what we can learn about mobs. There is a great deal there, actually, and if we pay the right kind of attention, we can profit more than a little bit.

When the Messiah was born into first-century Israel, He was born into a room full of fumes, ready to go off. It was politically volatile, and complicated, but it was also a complexity that could be reduced to two basic groups—those who had been baptized by John and those who had refused it.

So before we get to that reduction, we have to take a number of other factions into account. That way we know what we are reducing to *their* version of red state and blue state. There were the Sadducees, well connected to the aristocracy that controlled the Temple. They were theologically liberal but quite conservative when it came to their own vested interests. There were the Herodians, whose connections were to the political elite, and who had a deep investment in what Rome was seeking to maintain. The Pharisees were a lay renewal movement, highly respected among the people, at least until Jesus got done with them. There were about 6,000 Pharisees in Israel at this time. They were largely merchants who had made enough money to be able to retire to a life of personal devotion, their goal being to get the average Israelite to live up to the holiness standards that the Torah required of priests.

Let us (temporarily) exclude from this political roster the immediate followers of Christ—His twelve disciples, other extras, and the women in His entourage, but I am *not* excluding the *crowds* who loved Him, and who were not far from the kingdom. This was yet another group. Think of the massive crowds who welcomed Him during His Triumphal Entry. And as I never tire of saying, there is absolutely no reason for identifying this crowd with the mob that was yelling *crucify Him* a few days later. Jerusalem was big enough, and complicated enough, to have rival mobs.

But there is another group, almost always overlooked, a bit more surly and anti-establishment but still clearly in the pro-John-the-Baptist, pro-Jesus camp. This was a group of significant size that was hostile to the establishment that was hostile to Jesus. And by this I mean that they were seriously hostile, and at life-threatening levels. They were "on the Lord's side" but had not really internalized all that Sermon-on-the-Mount stuff. The Lord once rebuked a few of His disciples for not knowing what spirit they were of (Luke 9:55), but it should be pointed out that there was quite a large group out there who fit in the same category.

Let me introduce you to the Jesus mobs, and please bear with the repetition.

Jesus once asked His adversaries what they thought of John the Baptist. Remember what I said earlier about John the Baptist as a real dividing line.

> And they reasoned with themselves, saying, If we shall say, From heaven; he will say, Why then believed ye him not? But and if we say, Of men; *all the people will stone us*: for they be persuaded that John was a prophet. (Luke 20:5–6, emphasis added)

Jesus had cornered them by asking a question that forced them to choose between their own actions and the hostile reactions of a very hostile crowd. *All the people will stone us.* A few verses down from this, we see that the Jerusalem elites were plotting against Jesus, and they thought they needed to deal with Him secretly because why? Because they were afraid of the people. Jesus was really popular with a lot of people *who did not really grasp* the implications of what Christ had come to do: "And the chief priests and the scribes the same hour sought to lay hands on him; *and they feared the people*: for they perceived that he had spoken this parable against them" (Luke 20:19, emphasis added).

The gospel writers tell us this over and over. Two chapters later, the same thing is repeated: "And the chief priests and scribes sought how they might kill him; for *they feared the people*" (Luke 22:2, emphasis added).

In the gospel of Mark, the same thing is mentioned and emphasized.

> And the scribes and chief priests heard it, and sought
> how they might destroy him: for they feared him, be-
> cause all the people was astonished at his doctrine. . . .
> But if we shall say, Of men; *they feared the people*: for
> all men counted John, that he was a prophet indeed.
> (Mark 11:18, 32, emphasis added)

And in the next chapter of Mark, we see the same thing repeated: "And they sought to lay hold on him, *but feared the people*: for they knew that he had spoken the parable against them: and they left him, and went their way" (Mark 12:12, emphasis added).

And this same pattern does not disappear after the Lord ascended into Heaven. Not at all. When officials went to detain some apostles, they handled them quite gingerly. And why? *Because they feared for their lives.* "Then went the captain with the officers, and brought them without violence: for they feared the people, *lest they should have been stoned*" (Acts 5:26, emphasis added).

Now can we all agree that these crowds, as warmly affectionate toward John the Baptist as they might have been, and as doggedly committed to the honor of the rabbi Jesus as they were, were people who had not taken on board the full import of what the Scriptures required of them? I mean, had you gone to one of their rallies, who knows what kind of flags might have been there? And did their presence in the mix in any way discredit what Jesus was up to? Not even a little bit.

Did Andrew or Bartholomew ever need to feel a little sheepish and urge the Lord to issue a press release immediately to "denounce these unconscionable threats of violence"? Is there any hint of any of any weepy tweets from any of the Twelve, agonizing over how these Jesus mobs—ready to pick up stones, mind you—were making their BLM-friendly acquaintances feel?

No, the Lord knew of this group's cluelessness. He understood their cluelessness. He even used their cluelessness in His debates with that other form of cluelessness, the respectable kind. *The kind that is always the last to know.* But *He* never apologized for *their* cluelessness.

> And the Lord spake unto them, saying, "I have recently been informed that the chief priests have been receiving credible threats against their lives, and I wanted to hasten to apologize for any forms of violence that are being justified in my name. I would refer you to our most recent press release."

And just because we live in demented times, I need to remind you that I am not saying that Jesus said that. I am maintaining that He *didn't* say that.

So in this powder keg called Jerusalem, what did Jesus do? Did Jesus come in to pour soothing oil on troubled waters?

No, He went into the *Temple*, for crying out loud, and started flipping over tables.

I wonder if the respectable kind of clueless, the kind that is always the last to know, would have categorized the cleansing of the Temple and the storming of the Capitol as the same kind of thing. Actually I don't wonder at all. We call it the *cleansing* of the Temple, of course, because it is thousands of years in the past, and we read a bronze plaque about it in the Museum of Heroic Bygone Deeds. What would we call it if it had happened last week? Vandalism? Performance art? Prophecy without a permit?

And at this point someone is going to begin to *bluster hard*, and say, "You mean to say that you don't know the difference between Jesus and Viking Man?" And my reply is, "No, no, I am saying that *you* are the one who can't tell the difference. You are the head curator of Tombs of the Prophets Museum, and you are the one, if Jesus were here today, who would be demanding that *He* apologize for what Viking Man did." And Russell Moore would come out from the back ranks of the disciples and *try* to apologize for it, and then Jesus would shush him.

How do I know that you would demand that Jesus apologize for Viking Man? I mean, Jesus had nothing to do with it. Right. And neither did we, but you are demanding that *we* apologize for it.

☧

Given the events of the last few years, there are more than
a few disheartened secular conservatives out there. They see
the radical left growing in strength and influence, and they
know that unless it is somehow (miraculously) stopped, their
beloved America is done for. They see the squishy Republican establishment and wonder if they would ever be willing
to fight for *anything*. They see the soft evangelical "culturally
engaged" center lusting after the respect of the world, and
willing to lick dirt to get it. As an aside, licking dirt is not
a great strategy for gaining respect. They see the teeming
crowds that Trump attracted, like sheep without a shepherd,
and they wish that energy could be led but still don't want
anything to do with it.

To those who are in that position, I simply want to invite
you to come to Christ. Call upon Him and ask Him to
bring you to the Father. We can have no salvation without a Savior, no word without the Word, no transcendent
anchor without a Lord. And I want to ask you to consider
Christ, not only as the Lord of your life, but also as the
Lord of our public square.

☧

The alternative is militant atheism in the public square, and
by militant atheism I do not mean mild agnosticism. I mean
the savage gods of militant atheism. And if you have begun

to wonder, as you ought to have done, how "all this" could have happened in America, the answer is that *we turned our backs on Christ*. Because you have not trusted in Christ, the one who is Lord of all, you are part of the general apostasy, which means you are part of the problem. The left wants the apostasy and lusts after the consequences of the apostasy. The secular right wants the apostasy but doesn't really like the consequences. But America, like the prodigal son staring at an empty wallet, is now reckoning with the fact that the consequences have arrived regardless. So as part of your repentance, you need to acknowledge to the Father that *secular conservatism conserves nothing*.

Come to Christ, and do it now. He will receive and forgive you. We are fast approaching the point where real churches will be the only real resistance. Find and join one.

But not all churches are healthy. Don't join a diseased one.

There are two kinds of syncretism we must deal with. One of them is fairly obvious, at least to those outside the evangelical world of Trump Love. If you have a flag with Jesus on it, and Jesus is wearing a MAGA hat, then you fall into this category, and you need to put away your grotesque idols. You need to topple these small deities of an Americana amalgam. If your church year revolves around the Fourth of July, then this is your religion, which means that it is your damnation.

The other kind of syncretism looks at what I just wrote and mutters, "He's just saying that. He's just ticking the box. He's just 'yes butting.'" This is because the other kind of syncretism needs to be able to relegate *principled Christian conservatism*, which really is out there, and alive and well here in the pages of this book, to some category that can be easily dismissed by them, so they don't have to feel bad about *their* grotesque compromises. I won't itemize all their compromises, or give you a name for their overall project—but it rhymes with joke.

If in the name of racial reconciliation, you gave the old evangelical soft soap to the BLM riots, then apart from true repentance, you are on your way to Hell. I am tempted to say this because the people with their blasphemous Trump flags could use the company, but there is actually no such thing as "company" in the outer darkness. Still, it is all the same direction—a long, slow spiral into the abyss with no bottom.

Christian cultural engagement means "Jesus, Lord *over* everything in the world." It does not mean "Jesus *and* anything the world might be saying just now."

☩

Our cultural and political situation is a rocky and desolate moonscape. There are multiple groups and factions out here. There is a general clamor and a babble of voices. Some of them, faithful voices, believe that God has promised us that the moonscape will be restored to Eden again. The trees will be on both sides of the river, and the leaves will be for the healing of the nations (Rev. 22:2). It is possible for people who understand this, who do not trust in politics or in Trump, to see that the progressives are the current screaming threat to civic stability. And when the progressives by their tyrannies provoke various carnal reactions *elsewhere*, which they will continue to do, I am resolved not to feel apologetic over those reactions. Not even a little bit.

I am not one of the Twelve, or part of the Lord's inner circle. But I am one of those who lined the streets of Jerusalem, shouting *Hosanna* so many times I could scarcely talk the next day. And I was in the crowd listening that one time when the Lord asked those Temple johnnies, the ecclesiastical fat cats, whether the baptism of John was from Heaven or not. They twisted in the wind for about five minutes on that one, let me tell you! If they said that it was from Heaven, then He was going to follow up with, "Why didn't you get baptized by him then?" And if they said it was from men, then they were afraid of *"getting kilt"* by that surly lot just across from us—not our people, but, you know. Those guys.

In our day-to-day Christian walk, we all have to guard against double standards. It is a temptation that all of us are prone to. We must never attempt eye surgery on our brother, trying to get the speck out, when we have a beam in our own eye (Matt. 7:3–5). When we come to correct a brother, we have to remember ourselves, and consider ourselves, lest we also be tempted (Gal. 6:1). This should be part of ordinary Christian living. Do not expect others to cut you slack while at the same time cutting no slack for others. This is basic. Golden Rule. This is the law and the prophets.

We are not dealing with ordinary, life-in-the-village-level double standards. We are not even dealing with *egregious* double standards, as when those men were going to stone a woman for adultery (John 8:5) when they all were compromised by that same sin (John 8:9). They had enough remaining decency to feel ashamed and to tiptoe away. So I am not here discussing venial double standards, and not even talking about grotesque double standards.

No, what we are dealing with is double standards embraced openly, eagerly, relentlessly, flagrantly, and insolently, along with an impudent look that says *we dare you to say anything about it.* That is what the handlers of the left are orchestrating, and they know exactly what they are doing. This is what I mean by the *weaponization* of double standards. "If any of you shiny establishment Christians take any note of what we are doing out here in the noonday sun, we will promptly call you Trump-loving racists, and then where will you be? You misogynists."

The double standards are on display, on purpose. We are not *discovering* their double standards, as though they had been trying to hide them. They have been beating us over the head with their double standards for quite a while now, and they have been doing this because they want us to see

what they are doing and yet pretend as though we somehow didn't.

> Political correctness is communist propaganda writ
> small. In my study of communist societies, I came to
> the conclusion that the purpose of communist propa-
> ganda was not to persuade or convince, nor to inform,
> but to humiliate; and therefore, the less it corresponded
> to reality the better. When people are forced to remain
> silent when they are being told the most obvious lies,
> or even worse when they are forced to repeat the lies
> themselves, they lost once and for all their sense of pro-
> bity. To assent to obvious lies is to co-operate with evil,
> and in some small way to become evil oneself. One's
> standing to resist anything is thus eroded, and even de-
> stroyed. A society of emasculated liars is easy to control.
> I think if you examine political correctness, it has the
> same effect and is intended to.[1]

And this is being done in a such a way that the double
standards involved have been ramped up to a point where
they *cannot be missed*, kind of like those words that I just put
in all caps. They are unmistakable. And this is how we find
out who the cowards are. The cowards are those who will
not say what everybody sees and knows. The purpose of the

---

1. Theodore Dalrymple, "Frontpage Interview with Dr. Theodore Dalrymple:
Our Culture, What's Left of It," *Free Republic*, August 31, 2005.

glaring double standards is therefore to humiliate, and the deploying of these double standards is intentional.

But if we understand the biblical teaching about the Jesus mobs, we won't care about their double standards anymore. And that means the trick will no longer work.

☧

So all this is not happening because those conducting these continent-wide psych-ops are stupid or blind. No, it is being done so that *pretend* conservatives and *pretend* Christians will agree to *act* as though *they* were the stupid and blind ones. And many of them do it. Remember, the purpose is to humiliate.

It is as though a villain from a vintage western came up to one of our respectable guys, told him to dance, and started shooting at his feet. Later, when the humiliating and unfortunate incident was over, we tried to encourage that guy, because he was supposed to be our guy after all, and he said, "Oh, *no*. That's not it at all. Dance is very much part of our western cultural tradition, and we evangelicals have neglected it for far too long. I made sure to thank that gentleman for reminding me, in his rather direct way, of this important facet of our very imperfect heritage."

Few spectacles are sadder than all those *soi-disant* responsible Christians, the ones who have been chiding and rebuking me for years over my strictly Pauline views of slavery. Neither have they appreciated my understanding of what *actually* resulted from the War between the States. Their version of their concern is that I have been needlessly opening the Church up to unhelpful charges of *racccciiiisssm*. But you know what will *actually* condemn every last Christian as a vile and incorrigible racist? Just ten more birthdays, that's all.

The game that is being run on you people is plain and obvious, and you still refuse to see it. May the good Lord hasten the day when He gives you back your eyes.

So let us say that the Proud Boys do something that both you and your wife found to be less than enchanting. Not what you would have done. You did not do cartwheels when you heard about it. Should you feel terrible about your complicity? No. *Why should you?* You are not complicit.

We have to deal with these crowds, surging back and forth all around us. We might agree with something they do, we might be appalled by something else they do. We might debate with some of them, try to teach some of them, and call the cops on others. But we need not feel bad if we are right there in the middle of these tumultuous times, and we are actually part of a complicated Venn diagram. We need not feel bad about it, because we worship Almighty God on a weekly basis, in the name of Jesus Christ, and that is where our identity is.

As you do your level best before God to provide for and protect your family, you might find yourself in odd company sometimes. If you join a refugee column fleeing some deep blue weird diversity, it is quite possible that there is a crank conspiracy theorist somewhere else in that same refugee column. Should you feel bad about it? Crawl back to the people who made the refugee column necessary in order to seek their absolution and forgiveness? Not if you are a free man or free woman in Christ. I say this because the terms "man" and "woman" are terms that we have retained in our faith tradition, continuing to use them down to this day.

Jesus dealt with the crowds, in an ongoing way, and some of the crowds He dealt with were pretty dense. But we are followers of Christ, and the one thing He did *not* do with crowds is entrust Himself to them. So neither shall we.

> Now when he was in Jerusalem at the passover, in the feast day, many believed in his name, when they saw the miracles which he did. But Jesus did not commit himself unto them, because he knew all men, And needed not that any should testify of man: for he knew what was in man. (John 2:23–25)

And this is why we need to follow Christ, Christ above all. There is only one kind of defiant joy in the world that can successfully stand up to this kind of godless pressure. There is only one path for defying the screechers—without becoming a screecher yourself. That path is Christ, the one who has risen from the dead. And He rose from the dead in the same place where they crucified Him, which is to say, in the public square.

Remember: the reason Christians still own the public square is because Jesus rose from the dead in it. I know that the militant secularists despise this truth, but truth it is, and they should have thought of those objections before they crucified Him there.

And they somehow think that they can do something about that foundational and *drastic* mistake of theirs (1 Cor. 2:6–8) by dragging real believers out there and doing the same thing to them. Go right ahead. This is how Christ conquered the West the first time, and this is how He will do it again. Supplementing the blood of Abel will do nothing to silence the cries. When those guys start up with their pogroms targeting anyone who believes in a transcendent reality beyond the reach of their shaking fists, conservatives will start doing what they should have been doing all along—which is to say, going to church. *Real ones*, the kind that refuse to get a permit.

In the meantime, the Rev. Rabbitheart will have moved on, and now has a job with HR at Amazon, so you won't be able to try his church out. Just as well though.

> Christendom has had a series of revolutions and in each one of them Christianity has died. Christianity has died many times and risen again; for it had a God who knew the way out of the grave.[2]

2. G.K. Chesterton, *The Everlasting Man* (Moscow, ID: Canon Press, 2021), 273.

☧

Oh that thou wouldest rend the heavens, that thou wouldest come down, that the mountains might flow down at thy presence, as when the melting fire burneth, the fire causeth the waters to boil, to make thy name known to thine adversaries, that the nations may tremble at thy presence! (Isa. 64:1–2)

PART TWO

Mere Christendom

CHAPTER 5

What Is Mere Christendom?

So what do I mean by *mere Christendom* exactly?
I mean a network of nations bound together by a formal, public, civic acknowledgment of the Lordship of Jesus Christ, and the fundamental truth of the Apostles' Creed. I mean a public and formal recognition of the authority of Jesus Christ that repudiates the principles of secularism, and that avoids both hard sectarianism and easy latitudinarianism both. Easier said than done, but there it is. That is what we have to do, and we have to do it because secularism has run its course and does not have the wherewithal to resist the demands of radical Islam. Or a radical anything else, for that matter.

It is possible to argue for this without supporting an "established church," which—in the form of tax revenues—I do not support. But in order for this to happen at all, the Church must be established, in the sense that the magistrate has the responsibility to recognize her, to convene synods and councils to seek her counsel, and to listen to her. The magistrate himself has the responsibility, as a public figure, in the discharge of his office, to believe in Jesus, Lord of Heaven and earth.

As we proceed, remember that we must always hold on to the truth represented by "not whether, but which." It is not whether we will be governed by Christ, but rather which christ we will be governed by. The Lordship of Christ is not an option that we might select from a row of numerous options. It is Christ or chaos. It is Christ or Antichrist.

A word "God" that encompasses both the deity of Mormonism, who used to be a man just like us, and the triune Creator of Heaven and earth, worshiped by orthodox Christians, is for all intents and purposes a worthless word. It is a thin word, not a thick one.

Salvation for nations is religious, and it needs to be religiously thick. We cannot be saved by a thin religion. We cannot be saved by a religion the theological definitions of which will not stand up under five minutes of questioning. Etiolated faithy-words have no saving power. Why would they?

And, as it turns out, this problem goes back to John Adams. He rightly held that our republic was founded on "reason, morality, and the Christian religion" without "the monkery of priests." But though this was correct, Adams himself was beginning to move toward Unitarianism, the granddaddy of all the errors of American civic religion. Adams said that Christianity was necessary, at the very moment he was drifting out of it. But we need Jesus Christ, the only-begotten of the Father, raised for our justification, and we most certainly do not need a Generic Fomenter of Uplift in the Sky.

The mistake we made was this. If we want and need a "mere Christendom," then we need to keep that Christendom from becoming sectarian. That's one thing. But when you pour a diluting agent into your theology willy nilly, unless you take care, the dilution will affect the essential aspects of the Christian faith, like the death and resurrection of Jesus, and not just the relative unimportance of the debate between supralapsarians and infralapsarians.

Mere Christendom needs to be thin when it comes to the differences between Lutherans and Methodists, Presbyterians and Baptists, and so on. But it needs to manage to do this without thinning out the contents of the Apostles' Creed. It needs to be thick there.

Jesus is Lord. I have been arguing for years now that what is required is a return to Christendom, but in a form that I call mere Christendom. If you like, you can call it mere fundamentalism. A free civilization is necessarily larger than any of the Christian denominations within it, but at the same time a free civilization will have to be Christian. So I propose no single established church, no tax-supported denominations, but I do propose the formal adoption of the Apostles' Creed, and without any hermeneutical funny business. I propose that as a nation we formally confess together that Jesus actually did rise from the dead. If you protest that this would kill the great secular experiment that is America, I would reply that the great secular experiment that is America appears to have already gone out behind the barn and shot itself already.

The libertarian aspect of this insists that most of our practical problems can be addressed through repealing laws and abolishing agencies. When most people hear about a "theocratic" anything, they assume they will soon be confronted with ayatollah-manned death panels. But all societies are theocratic, with the only thing distinguishing them being the nature and attributes of the reigning *theos*. Since our current *theos* happens to be a bloodthirsty maniac, and because I am not a devotee of that particular religion, I would urge my fellow citizens to turn away from him and turn to our heavenly Father.

The first thing that would happen in a biblical law order is that the EPA, the IRS, the Department of Education, etc. would all be abolished. Legitimate functions of government (Defense, State, etc.) would be significantly downsized or redirected.

The positive laws I would like to see enacted would be in the area of constitutional process and reform. The kind of government we are currently abused by is precisely the kind of government that our Constitution was originally drafted to prevent. Consequently I would like to see reform primarily undertaken through "process" laws instead of "content" laws. By this I mean laws of process restraining our rulers, and not any new laws governing the peons.

A good example would be term limits, or a law requiring "none of the above" on every ballot, such that if "none of the above" wins, a new election with new candidates be scheduled. The goal should be to have a government that stays within its appointed bounds. The goal should be to keep the termites out of the woodwork.

A formal recognition of the Lordship of Jesus is necessary but not sufficient. More is required than paper commitments. All true constitutions arise from the people, and genuine allegiance to Christ is not going to happen unless there is a reformation and revival. In order for any of this to work, we must have countless preachers of the gospel, faithfully declaring the death, burial, and resurrection of Christ. The role of the government here is to stay out of the way, allowing such preachers free access to the people, and thereby encouraging them to have at it. If you don't give a heck about the man with the Bible in his hand, as the Staple Singers taught us, just "get out the way and let the gentleman do his thing." There is a straight line blessing that runs from free grace to free men, and from free men to free markets.

Culture wars should be fought in the culture, not in the courts. One of the central reasons for having a constitutionally limited government is so that one cultural faction does not get to cheat, using the force of law to skew the outcomes in their favor. Since law is coercive by definition, the areas in which coercion is allowed should be radically limited. The law should protect life, liberty, and property. After that, the alternative visions for truth, goodness, and beauty may freely compete. Using their own money, voluntarily donated, the secularists and atheists may build their own schools, write poems and novels, produce plays and movies, build cathedrals, compose concertos, and so on.

But it will not have escaped your notice that such free competition is a *Christian* value, and by limiting government in this way we have already decided what is the best way for everyone. There is no neutrality. So I don't want liberty for secularists because secularism is true—it isn't. Secularism is an opium dream, complete with flashing eyes and floating hair. I want liberty for secularists because Jesus is Lord. Because Jesus is Lord, the right of fallen sinners to wield coercive power must be strictly limited. One of the toughest lessons for sinners to learn is the necessity of leaving other sinners alone. When we do not leave them alone—in cases of rape and murder, for example—we have express warrant from God to do so. We do not have express warrant from God to make secularists confess something they don't believe.

Biblical masculinity is cultural gluten. Without it, the cookie just crumbles to pieces in your hand, and is tasteless on top of that. Or someone at the organic equivalent of DuPont comes up with an artificial bonding agent that either doesn't work or turns the cookie into an all-natural shower tile.

What are we to say of those Christian leaders who are masculine enough to want to be in leadership, but not biblically masculine enough to accept the assigned sacrifices that go with it? One of the central sacrifices is this—one who assumes authority in the kingdom must be willing to be the drudge servant of the others (Matt. 23:11–12). But after three years with Jesus, the disciples got into a quarrel on the road to Jerusalem about who would be the greatest (Mark 9:33). After three years with Jesus, the disciples were disputing among themselves *at the Last Supper* about who would be large and in charge (Luke 22:24). Does anybody honestly think that the leadership of the North American evangelical church is free of this temptation that repeatedly snared the disciples?

☧

I am fond of quoting Chesterton's great observation that the one taste of paradise on earth is to fight in a losing cause, and then not lose it. That prospect is before us now. But *where* do we go to fight? Where is the center of the fight? There are various aspects to this question, but one of the more obvious is that in order to be the center of the fight, there has to be fighting. As the fellow once said, this ain't beanbag.

Without Christ, nothing holds together (Col. 1:17–18). But in order to be an active part of His kind of bonding, leaders have to be more than hirelings (John 10:12). They have to be gifts from Christ to His people, and in order to be complete gifts from Him, they need to be more like Him. But we need to be done with leaders who want to be like Jesus, only not so bloody.

When that gracious gift is finally given, then God will raise up leaders who can look at the chaos of our battlefield and see a straight-line path to victory. If God does not give it, then our particular cause is lost, and see you in the resurrection. We can look at all the game film then—and we will be able to handle *that* because there will be no tears there (Rev. 21:4). Whatever the case, we are well past the point of being able to save ourselves. We have to quit pretending.

As Tozer once put it, if revival means more of what we have now, we most certainly do not need revival.

☧

One of the more notable features of the life of our Lord, as recorded in Scripture, is the fact that references to the outside world are overwhelmingly political. When Jesus was born, Augustus was Caesar (Luke 2:1) and Quirinius was governor of Syria (Luke 2:2). Herod the Great was ruler in Judea (Luke 1:5) and wielded his power to the grief of many mothers in Bethlehem. Tiberius was Caesar when John the Baptist began his ministry (Luke 3:1–2), and Luke includes a number of interesting names when he dates the arrival of the forerunner of the Messiah. Tiberius was still emperor when Jesus died, and this political orientation is sealed by the fact that Pontius Pilate was included in the Apostles' Creed.

The New Testament is silent when it comes to the other outside celebrities. We are told very little about their poets, their actors, their singers. We know little of their architects from the pages of the New Testament, even though they had magnificent architects. No, Scripture focuses on the political rulers, and this is because it is where the fundamental challenge was mounted.

If we may speak so, Herod was a prophetic unbeliever, a man of despotic insight. He learned from the magi that a king was born among the Jews and consulted with his scribes on the assumption that this was the Christ (Matt. 2:1–2). The magi simply saw a king—a scepter would arise in Israel, and a star would rise in Jacob (Num. 24:17). They took the revelation they had been given with simple delight and brought treasures to the young king. But Herod, the moment he heard of it, knew that he was dealing with a *rival*, and he acted accordingly.

He was wrong in the side he chose, but he was not wrong in the facts of the case. Jesus saw Himself as a rival to the world's way of running things. He would not receive the kingdoms of the earth from the devil's hand, and He refused because He intended to be Messiah the Prince, the Prince of His Father, and not the prince of the dark archon. And He was a rival to every form of ungodly rule from the first moment He took breath. Though we call it a silent night, this suckling child was actually the deafening shout of God's defiance. The principalities and powers, the thrones and dominations, were all going to come to nothing.

And so He was born in our midst, Immanuel, God with us, the one who was to become King of all kings, and Lord of all lords.

When Jesus assumed human nature, He did so first as a single cell. The eternal Word of the eternal Father, the one who spoke the heavens and earth into existence, took on a body that was the size of the period at the end of this sentence. His intent was to redeem every aspect of human existence, and so He did it by assuming it all. He was a baby, a toddler, a young boy, a teenager, and a man. He did all this as a way of receiving us back into fellowship with Him. He was redeeming what He was taking on. He was taking on human nature, and so it was that He was redeeming human nature. When He saves us, He receives us. But as a result, when He saves us, we receive Him. And when we receive what He assumed to Himself, which was a mortal body, we are in fact receiving a cosmos remade. There is no way to receive the child in the manger without receiving what that child was given, which is all rule and authority, dominion and power, world without end.

This leaves us with a choice. If we receive Him, we are also receiving what He received. When we welcome this child, we of necessity must welcome the children. There is no way to welcome the Lord without also welcoming His dominion.

And this is why the perennial, constant choice is always between Christ and Herod. Either the children are brought to Christ so that He might bless them, or soldiers go out from Herod so that they might slay them. It is either the blood of Christ, redeeming the children of men, or it is the blood of the children of men, polluting the thrones of men. There is no other way, no other option. If you will not have Christ-sons for rulers, then you have made your choice— you will have the Herod-apes for rulers.

Whenever we talk about the "true meaning of Christmas," we must always keep this truth immediately before us. The central Christian message has always been that *Jesus is Lord.* We celebrate His birth because He was born among us in order to become Lord. Now that He has been established in that rule, we can commemorate His birth because we also remember to commemorate His coronation. Without the Ascension, Christmas is nothing.

Our civilization has made this choice, in an appalling direction, toward the abyss of a bottomless damnation. Like ancient Carthage, we pretend to ground our liberties on the blood sacrifice of living children.

And so we Christians repurpose the repeated message of Cato the Elder: the true message of Christmas is *Carthago delenda est*—Carthage must be destroyed.

But remember where we began. This will not happen to nameless functionaries and bureaucrats. Christ is born, the angels sing, the shepherds became the first evangelists, the magi came and worshiped. A particular king named Herod felt the presence of a rival and marshaled his forces. Those forces are still present in the world today, and they are ordered about by men and women with names. We still have a large portion of our task before us—the nations of men must still be discipled. But until they are, we declare the Christian message, the Christmas message, to men with faces and names.

We know the names of Jesus and His enemies. We do not know the names of the magi. They submitted and bowed low, and so their names will wait until the resurrection to be declared.

Until then we declare the name of the one raised in the great resurrection, the only resurrection ever to happen in the middle of history, and because we name the name of the risen Jesus, we are simultaneously declaring a victory and defeat. The kingdoms of this world have become the kingdoms of our God and of His Christ, and He shall reign forever and ever. That is the victory. The names of all who hate and oppose Him will fall and be forgotten forever. That is their ignominious defeat. I could name thousands of such, from every political faction, but will content myself with only one proper name—these are all represented by their covenant head, Joe Biden. He, and the way of governance he represents, is *necessarily* stained with the blood of children. The only alternative is to be cleansed with the blood of the Child.

Therefore, the message of Christmas is that we are saved by the blood of the Child, and never by the blood of children. And if we are saved by the blood of the Child, it then becomes possible (and necessary) for our children to be saved, together with the rest of us.

CHAPTER 6

A Brief Scattershot Primer on Christian Nationalism

W e should begin with the recognition that naming is warfare. In any cultural collision, each group wants to name the other one, and each group wants to prevent the other group from taking that name and turning it around to be used in a less pejorative sense, or even in a positive sense. *Methodist* and *Puritan* were originally names that were taunts from outside those communities, but were soon enough rendered innocuous. In our day, the mud-gobbing that calls conservative Christians names like *white supremacist*, or *theo-fascist*, or *religious extremist* is so overdone that it is easily answered and then dismissed. Some are so out there that they can simply be answered with a cheerful roll of the eyes. But another taunt they are now using—Christian nationalist—can be easily caught and thrown right back to them. I am a Christian, and I do love my nation. Now what?

I am a Christian, and I am not a globalist. I am a Christian, and I am not a tribalist. I am a Christian, and I have to live somewhere. What shall we call that?

Understood rightly, Christian nationalism relates to mere Christendom the same way that a brick relates to a brick wall. It relates to mere Christendom the same way that an egg relates to an omelet. It relates the same way that different colored yarns relate to the sweater.

The one possible toxin in the phrase *Christian nationalism* is found in that pesky suffix *–ism*. As the fellow said, beware all *isms* except for prisms. Christian conservatives are hostile to ideologies, and "Christian nationalism" *can* be made to function in such a troublesome ideological way. But if we take care to define our terms and guard our hearts against the poison of party spirit, we should be all right.

But those on the right who gladly welcome sobriquets like Christian nationalist, but who then receive it like it was the very latest blasphemous selection from the fruit-of-the-month club, with all the cherries, my only word to them is that they should repent and knock it off. Just a word. Driving your pick-up around town with that huge Trump flag flapping on one side and the Let's Go Brandon in the original Greek waving on the other . . . isn't helping anything.

A *Christian* nation should never be mistaken as being the same thing as a *chosen* nation. There is no exceptionalism in it. In the Old Testament era, Israel was God's chosen nation, and the other nations were not. But in the era of the new covenant, the commandment that Christ left for us meant that we were to disciple *all* the nations. The first Christian nation (which was probably Armenia) was not an only child. She was simply the eldest, knowing that there were going to be lots of other kids. And as that family fills out, God doesn't want us squabbling about which one is the greatest, any more than Jesus wanted His disciples to argue about that same thing on the road to Jerusalem. So the "American exceptionalism" of the neocons is actually the idolatrous construct. What we are urging is simply one more Christian nation among many, and to God be the glory.

Secular nationalism recognizes no authority above itself, and hence it is in essence idolatrous. Christian nationalism recognizes a transcendental authority over all nations, an authority that is before time, above history, and entirely outside the world, and which views all of our haughtiness as risible Ozymandian hubris. "Behold, the nations are as a drop of a bucket, and are counted as the small dust of the balance: behold, he taketh up the isles as a very little thing" (Isa. 40:15).

In the meantime, down here on earth, you cannot teach children to have respect for other cultures by inculcating in them a contempt for their own. A son who honors his own mother deeply is going to understand why another honorable son wants to honor *his* mother. That makes good sense to him. A man who loves his American heritage in the proper way is going to understand and appreciate it when an Englishman loves his, and a Korean loves his, and an Israeli loves his, and an Argentinian loves his. *As they are all supposed to.* Those who attempt to tear down respect for our own institutions are actually setting in motion a contempt for all institutions everywhere, and so then no one should be surprised when an alumnus of this multicultural curricular farrago heads down to their *alma mater* in order to shoot up the cafeteria. While it is true that both jingoism and nihilism start at home, so does respect. Respect and honor are learned when kids are little, and if you fail to teach them at that point, you are the one graduating fascists and anarchists.

Mere Christendom is not Christian nationalism. Mere Christendom is the sum total of lots of smaller Christian nationalisms.

If we were in the business of using red baseball caps as a way of spreading our views, we would not opt for the MAGA hat. Our adversaries are trying to fit us out for a MAC hat—Make America Christian. Our reply to this is that if we are going to say it with hats, we would come up with a MACA hat— Make America Christian *Again*. I italicize *again* for a reason.

The thing we are trying to accomplish is not an attempt to square the circle. It has been done before. In fact, it has been done multiple times before. The first Christendom had a run of over a thousand years, which I call pretty good.

And not only has this Christian nationalism thing been
done before, it has been done in *America* before. If we succeed, this will not be Christian America. If we succeed, this
will be Christian America 2.0. This will be Christian America *again*. This will be America as the prodigal son, tired of
the pig food, coming home to his father.

Unlike the French Revolution, which erased the Christian
calendar in order to plonk down their own humanist version, the U.S. Constitution was drafted in the year of our
Lord 1787. The Declaration acknowledged our rights are
inalienable precisely because they were bestowed on us by
our *Creator*. When the Constitution was adopted, nine of
the thirteen states had official ties to a Christian denomination. Connecticut had an established Congregational church
down to the 1830s. Whatever else you say about church
establishments at the state level (and there *is* room for crit-
icism), you cannot say that it is unconstitutional. Out of the
fifty-five men at the Constitutional Convention, fifty of them
were orthodox Christians. In one survey of the political lit-
erature of the founding era, it was determined that the apostle Paul was quoted at the same level as were Montesquieu
and Blackstone, and Deuteronomy was quoted *twice as much*
as John Locke was.[1] One of the names those in England had

---

1. David Dreisbach, *Reading the Bible with the Founding Fathers* (New York:
Oxford University Press, 2017), 66.

for the American Revolution was "the Presbyterian Revolt," and on the floor of Parliament Horace Walpole said that "cousin America has run off with a Presbyterian parson," referring to Witherspoon. Speaking of Witherspoon, that worthy man signed the Declaration, and he counted James Madison among his students.

Everyone who subscribes to the Westminster Confession of Faith is a Christian nationalist. This even applies to the American version of the Westminster, which muted the high-octane Christian nationalism of the original British version. In the original it says that it is the duty of the magistrate "to take order that unity and peace be preserved in the Church, that the truth of God be kept pure and entire, that all blasphemies and heresies be suppressed, all corruptions and abuses in worship and discipline prevented or reformed, and all the ordinances of God duly settled, administered, and observed" (WCF 23.3). This was a bit thick for the American Presbyterians, who held their first General Assembly in Philadelphia in 1789, electing a gent named Witherspoon to be their moderator, and who modified the Westminster to say this: "Yet, as nursing fathers, it is the duty of civil magistrates to protect the Church of our common Lord, without giving the preference to any denomination of Christians above the rest, in such a manner that all ecclesiastical persons whatever shall enjoy the full, free, and unquestioned liberty of discharging every part of their sacred functions, without violence or danger" (American Westminster 23.3). Also please note: Isaiah's nursing fathers, Church of our common Lord, Witherspoon, Philadelphia, 1789. These people were all breathing the same air.

If you know any PCA ministers who are woke, or semi-woke, or just simply political squishes, try not to rib them too much about all this stuff. They probably feel bad enough about it already, especially since they have had *so* many opportunities to take an exception to the American Westminster, at who knows how many meetings of presbytery, and yet they refused to distance themselves from this element of their theo-fascist past. They are probably wracked with guilt over this confessional issue anyhow, and we should probably just lay off.

One last thing. There is no such entity as the Judeo/Christian religion. As *religions* go, there is no way to combine the view that Jesus is the Christ with the idea that He was a fraud, or the claim that He rose from the dead with the counterclaim that He did nothing of the kind, or the idea that the New Testament correctly interprets the Old with the view that it is the Talmud that actually does. So as *religions*, they do not harmonize at the most basic level.

But what then is the Judeo/Christian tradition? Orthodox Christianity and orthodox Judaism both make transcendental claims, claims that outrank the pretensions of
modern secular man. The Judeo/Christian *tradition* was
therefore a device used by secular man to get Christians
and Jews to drop or mute their claims about that authority being from outside the world. This follows because if
you establish this amalgam tradition down here when the
transcendental claims are contradictory, then that means
you don't need to take either Christianity or Judaism seriously as a basis for governance. You have spiked the transcendental guns. The Judeo/Christian tradition therefore
operates from within the system, and for a number of years
has occupied an honored spot on secular man's designated
god shelf—mementos and knickknacks from the past. A
Judeo/Christian lapdog cannot stand up to the secular
onslaught, because the Judeo/Christian lapdog was first
domesticated by secularism, and it has been that way for
a long time. So while conservative Christians and conservative Jews can certainly work together to challenge the
current threats posed by humanist man, they must do so
without kidding themselves—as co-belligerents, as distinct
from allies. In order to do this with any kind of consistency,
they must both recover an understanding of the transcendental nature of their own central claims. But then again,
these ultimate claims are not consistent with each other.
So the best thing that could happen at this point would be

for conservative Jews to reconsider, seriously, the claims of Christ the Messiah.

And of course, everybody else should do that too.

CHAPTER 7

The Goodness of Mere Christendom

C hristians who try to evade the force of the "not whether, but which" argument will sometimes resort to saying it is the "best" system without saying where they are deriving their understanding of what *best* means.

So Christians who argue for a secular public square are caught on the horns of a dilemma. Either Jesus wants this or He doesn't. Or maybe He doesn't care. If He doesn't want it, then why do they? If He does, then are they not advocating a civil arrangement based on the will of the Lord, which would be a theocracy?

When we are talking about a theocracy in the abstract, we are not yet talking about the content of the laws, only that the laws are based on the will of God. Biblical law, rightly understood, would *not* be draconian, but that needs to be discussed in its place. Right now, the question is simply whether or not public morality needs to be grounded in the will of God or not.

So let's take this a step further. If the laws are not based on the will of God, but rather on the will of the people, Demos, then what happens when a large majority of the people think that the laws should be based on the will of a god? This is precisely the dilemma that democracy faces in the Middle East. The president of Turkey has said that democracy is like a street car—you ride it until your stop. *Then you get off.* What happens when an Islamic state forms as a result of democratic processes? What happens when Hamas actually wins the election in Gaza, and they didn't do it by cheating?

In effect, Demos the capricious god gives way to another god. But on secularist principles, why would Demos not have the right to abdicate like this? Who says that Demos can't abdicate?

When a Christian secularist looks at this kind of scenario, if Demos is the final word, then cannot Demos vote itself out of having the final word? Can it not enthrone Allah? If Allah is not the true God, can it not, at any rate, enthrone the mullahs?

Or what about Jesus? On what basis could a Christian secularist object to an election that voted in Jesus as Lord? He could only do it by saying that Jesus refused to be nominated and then by pointing to a text that showed us how Jesus required our civil affairs to be arranged, and that He was particularly insistent that we be sure to leave Him out of it. But the whole point for the secularist is that there is no such text, which, ironically, opens the door for a democratic Christian republic.

Now of course, I believe that Jesus is actually a king, not a president, and the Great Commission requires us to proclaim that the coronation has already happened. Jesus is not running for anything, and we do not "make" Him anything. He is the Lord of lords, the King of kings, and the President of presidents, and there is nothing whatever that we can do about it. That is already the case. The world will gradually come to recognize this, and will become Christian, and this is good news indeed. This is *the* good news.

This is incidentally why I believe that Christian republics and commonwealths are formed by preaching, baptizing, and discipleship, and not by campaigning, legislating, pundit-blogging, and so on. This gospel work will have political results, but it is not politically established. The magistrate is a necessary part of the process, but only as a servant to the gospel. The magistrate must wear Christ's livery, and not the other way around.

So here are the options: (1) Jesus doesn't care whether or not nations are explicitly Christian. (2) Jesus is opposed to nations being explicitly Christian. (3) Jesus wants nations to be explicitly Christian.

And here should be our responses to these possibilities:
(1) Well, if Jesus doesn't care, that means we have the right
to care. So let's make this a Christian nation, shall we? (2)
Okay. Let's have a Bible study and find out why "disciple the
nations" really means "don't disciple the nations, whatever
you do." (3) Yes, Lord.

☧

The notion of mere Christendom is not just a personal pipe
dream. It is not a collection of "wouldn't it be nice" surmises.
A Reformed understanding of the gospel, of worship, of education, of politics, and so on, is incoherent apart from a commitment to Christendom. Christendom is an essential part
of a Reformed theology in its historical setting. This does
not mean that said Christendom must be up and already
running—just that there needs to be a commitment to it by
faith. When Abraham saw his descendants as heirs of the
whole world, and not by law either (Rom. 4:13), he did not
have Christendom up and running at just that moment. But
he still knew that the world was his, and that his heirs would
walk around in it.

A faithful Reformed missionary in Egypt knows that
Christendom is not right outside his window. But *Jesus* is
right outside his window, and everywhere else too. We do not
yet see everything subject to man—but we see *Jesus*. Christendom will be easier to see when it can be photographed, but
we are called to see it whether it can be photographed or not.

☧

This whole issue is what systematic theologians might call a "big deal." Underneath a lot of the current controversies that are roiling the Reformed world are the issues of paedocommunion and postmillennialism. The thing these two doctrines share in common is that they are both, in different ways, *an optimistic testimony about the course of future generations.*

Paedocommunion nurtures the next generation in optimistic faith, and postmillennialism is the grounded hope that God will continue to nurture His Church across multiple generations. Generations do not occur in the resurrection—they are a phenomenon found in *this* world, and they are directly connected to the questions that swirl around the formation of a culture. No culture without *cultus*. A culture is religion externalized, and thus it makes sense to ask of every culture what form of worship lies at the center of it. It is a stark fact that the center of secular culture is *not* the worship of God the Father through the name of Jesus, in the power of the Holy Spirit. That being the case, Christians ought to have no devotion whatsoever to secular culture. Devotion to their culture means devotion somehow to their gods, and we should always refuse to bow down to their gods.

If this historic Reformed faith is resurgent (and it is), and if people are starting to pay attention to it (and they are), and this poses a threat to those in the Reformed world who have signed a peace treaty with the Amalek . . . I meant to say the secular state, then it might seem like a good idea to distract everybody by getting people to be suspicious about our Reformed *bona fides*.

This can easily be done by saying that we are wobbly at best on *sola fide*, or that we are sacramentalists of some sort, and that such things are clearly Not Good. But if they were to raise the real objection, which is that we believe that Jesus is Lord of Heaven and earth, and that the earth ought to admit it sooner rather than later, a lot of people in their own churches would wonder (and perhaps say), "What's wrong with that?" It is easier to say that we don't really preach the gospel than to say something far closer to the truth, which is that we believe that the unchained gospel is in the process of conquering the whole world.

After all, how potent is a gospel that allows you the freedom to sign peace treaties with Amalekites?

☧

There is a sense in which (I have argued) every thoughtful Christian must be a conservative. The Holy Spirit has done a lot thus far in the history of our people, and we must live up to what we have already attained. We must *conserve* it. There is another sense in which we are to be progressive— the Holy Spirit has a lot yet left to do in the history of this world. We must *progress* towards it.

But unlike that unruly tribe we call progressives, Christian progressives are looking for that city whose maker and builder is God. We know where we are going, and we don't just exult (as they do) in the fact that we are making good time, and who knows where. And unlike the secularist conservatives, we are not in love with the existing evils, prepared to fight off every attempt to replace them with other evils.

So there is a sense in which the Christian faith is both conservative and progressive, and yet another sense in which it is neither. The Christian faith is inescapably political, but it must not allow itself to be co-opted by secular and unbelieving partisanship. And to reject partisanship is to reject compromises with secularists who want to hook up with an evangelical voting bloc.

But the necessary rejection of partisanship is *not* a rejection of particularity. There are times when every faithful Christian must vote for this candidate and against that one, pray for the success of this referendum and for the defeat of that one.

There is an expressed desire to keep the gospel "unfettered," which is actually a desire to have an Obama-like gospel—always there, and always voting "present." You see, if the gospel requires us to say and do something *particular*, then enemies of the gospel can always accuse us of being in cahoots with some secularist organization that has said something very similar to that particular thing. And thus they can steer us with ease.

We can't say anything particular, because there is always a group out there that we could be falsely identified with. According to them, we must preach an *unfettered* gospel, by which we mean a floaty thing above all our heads, which will guarantee that those little floaty things that we call our souls will, shortly after we die, ascend up to that Euclidean floaty place called Gnostic Heaven. There we will have great fellowship with those giants of the faith—Cerinthus, Carpocrates, Basilides, and Valentinus. *Ecclesia deformata et semper deformanda.*

You see, if the gospel says that repentance and belief actually mean something in *this* world—like canceling that sex change operation, or forgoing the nuptials with someone whose genitalia are uncannily similar to yours, or letting your kid stay alive, or even worse, having a repentant king say that such goings-on ought not to be going on—such particulars might create a stumbling block. No stumbling blocks! We must preach an unfettered message of repentance, by which we mean that we must thunder a message that every man must repent of "stuff." Like what? You know, *stuff.*

Suppose the point were to be made—and it is a worthy point to make—that being a Christian trumps being an American. This is a point with which I am in whole-hearted agreement, and which I have made in my writing numerous times. A conservative Republican believer in Jesus has far more in common with a Palestinian Christian than he does with a secular representative of the state of Israel. A thousand amens. Jesus makes all the difference.

But there is a way of agreeing with this that shows one is growing up into the fundamental tenets of "mere Christendom," and there is another way of agreeing with it that shows one is just becoming a liberal. There is a way of appealing to Jesus because you find Jesus appealing, and there is a way of appealing to Jesus because you find American hegemony unappealing.

So here is a litmus test for you. I am afraid it is an unpopular litmus test because it works every time. It is *that* kind of unpopular.

If you find yourself in real solidarity with Palestinian Christians, and you want to know if it is love for Jesus, or just your nascent inner-anti-Semite rising, just ask yourself this question, which, in its theological structure is exactly the same question. Who do you have more in common with—a Palestinian *non*-Christian or a devout Christian woman with hoop earrings who just got back from the RNC, where she spent the entire convention wearing a big hat shaped like an elephant?

I said it is exactly the same question, and it is. The reason we might get radically different answers is that something else is going on. There is a lot of "radical" Christianity out there that is just a pretense—it is simply a stalking horse for another tired form of anti-Americanism. Show me something new.

I say all this knowing that there is a prophetic case to be made against America's sins, which are great, and I know further that it is our duty in the Church to make that case. I know also that the heavy gravitational pull of various American idolatries has many conservative believers trapped in a crisscross spider web of red, white, and blue. But *faux*-solidarity with Christians on the other side of the world is nowhere near escape velocity. If shared love for Jesus can transcend the barriers thrown up by the conflict in the Middle East, then why can't it transcend the barriers created by your neighbor's love for *The 700 Club*, and your inability to abide that man?

It turns out that love for Jesus, of this sort anyway, only creates solidarity if we know next to nothing about a situation. We have created our own version of Linus's maxim—"I love mankind. It's people I can't stand." We say, "I love Palestinian Christians. It's dispensational Zionist Southern Baptist Christians I can't stand." And it turns out that the whole thing hinges on the fact that you actually know some people in this latter group. And their entire outlook and demeanor (and support for Israel!) means loving them constitutes a whole new level of Christian discipleship. Might as well get started.

So our task is to proclaim the crown rights of King Jesus, an imperial authority that is not based on raw diktat, but rather on His shed blood that forgives every sin it comes in contact with. But it is important to note that it comes in contact with sin in places others than the individual human heart. It does that, too, of course, but the blood of Jesus deals with the sins of Congress, the Supreme Court, and the President.

The blood of Jesus purchased every state legislature, and the surrounding grounds, out to the sidewalks. The blood of Jesus purchased every major New York publishing house. We should tell them. The blood of Jesus owns every art form and has all movie rights. We should tell them too. The blood of Jesus is mixed into the mortar that holds the true cornerstone. It is the only real basis for any future civilization. There are no other real options.

Which means there is therefore no way to preach the blood of Christ without advancing the sacrificial glory of the next Christendom.

CHAPTER 8

Church and State

An argument for mere Christendom must not be mistaken for an attempt to get back to the church/state relations as they existed in the medieval period. An argument for mere Christendom is not an argument for some sort of ecclesiocracy. A good approach to these issues was worked out in the Reformation era, with its development of what might be called the historic two-kingdoms understanding, over against a very recent distortion of that doctrine.

In my various discussions of the *modern* forms of "two kingdom" theology, I have frequently summed up my concerns with the question of how many *kings* there are. This has made my point, to a point, but it still needs to be pushed into the corners.

Here is my summary of what I take to be a theological novelty, by which I am referring to the R2K position, and the position I am interacting with.

> God rules all human institutions and endeavors, but He does so in two fundamentally different ways. He rules in His spiritual kingdom, the Church, as a redeemer, and He rules the civil realm as Creator and sustainer. These two kingdoms have different ends and functions, and therefore, they must be ruled differently. The spiritual kingdom is governed by special revelation, the Bible, and the other kingdom is governed by natural law.

I take this to be a novelty because, according to the Reformers, the spiritual kingdom was that of the heart, the conscience, the inner man, while the other kingdom was external and visible, Church included (e.g., Calvin's *Institutes*, 3.19.15). In other words, this modern form of it divides Church and state while the reformational form of it divided inner and outer, invisible and visible.

So with all that noted, here are my basic questions for adherents of the modern take on two kingdoms. Assuming the divide is between civil and ecclesiastical . . .

1.   Is there anything in the charter of each kingdom that prohibits cooperation, communication, and traffic with the other kingdom? In other words, does natural law reveal that we must not ever resort to

special revelation? And does special revelation ever say that we must never import specific and revealed content into the civil realm?

2. As God rules in the civil realm, does He require us to worship Him? If not, why not? If so, under what name, and by what forms? Or in this realm is He satisfied with being the unknown god of the Athenians? Or was an altar to Him too much? Is the God mentioned on American coinage the God of natural law?

3. As God rules in the civil kingdom as Creator and sustainer, does our human disobedience of natural law also mean that He acts in His capacity as judge? Using the criteria of natural law alone, will God judge us for our abortion laws, same-sex mirages, and confiscatory taxation?

4. If God can act as judge in the civil realm, is there any gospel or good news for those under judgment in this realm? If He does not act as judge in this realm, in what sense can He be said to be ruling?

5. If the reason for not bringing special revelation to bear in discussions about what to do in the civil realm is that unbelievers don't believe the Bible, what are we to do in those debates when they claim not to believe in natural law either? If their denials and unbelief do not cause us to set aside natural law,

then why should their denials and unbelief be the
cause for us to set aside the Scriptures?

I have written elsewhere on the ideal relationship of Church
and kingdom, comparing it to the church at the center of
town, and life in the kingdom fanning out into the parish
from that center. Word and sacrament are at the center, and
they shape and form the lives of believers outside the sanctuary, but without ruling and dictating what goes on out there.
I am using the words *sanctuary* and *parish* in a figure. The
elders of the Church do not rule over auto mechanics, or
garbage collection, or interior design. First, it is none of their
business, and secondly, they would do a bad job.

Family government and civil government and Church government are the three governments ordained and established
directly by God. Our task is therefore to make sure they are in
a right relationship with each other, and to take care that one
of them doesn't try to swallow up the others. In our day, it is
the state that is swollen with this particular conceit, but other
eras have seen the other two governments try it.

After the Great Commission is fulfilled, it would be
appropriate, in a figure of speech, to say that "the Church"
has filled the earth, as the waters cover the sea, but this is not
talking about the Church in the strict sense—gathered worship, the preached Word, the bread and wine, etc. A great
deal of what will have been done by that point will have been

done by nations and by families. These nations and families will have been baptized, and they will return to the sanctuary every Lord's Day to be instructed and strengthened, but they will do what they do as *Christians*—not as officers of the sanctuary.

So that's the background.

Let's take a test case. I used the phrase "shape and form" to talk about the kind of influence the sanctuary has on the parish, and a good example of this kind of thing from the New Testament would be the case of role relationships between men and women. It is good for two reasons—the first is that there is abundant material in Scripture about it. Secondly, the issue has that peculiar kind of clarity that will cause the enemies of the truth to get whipped up into a bubbly froth, and the trimmers of the truth to hem, cough, and dig a little divot in the carpet with their shoe.

What I want to argue is that the rule of the sanctuary is authoritative in how it shapes us, but it does this in organic ways. It is not done by rules made out of two-by-fours. That shaping authority is applied out in the world by men and women with brains.

To jump back to my illustration of auto mechanics, a preacher has no business telling a mechanic how to repair a blown head gasket. He can tell him that he must charge in accordance with the bid he made, and that he may not take financial advantage of a little old lady who knows nothing about cars. The sanctuary influences the auto shop without becoming the owner or proprietor of it.

When the Church is healthy, and doing what it ought to be doing, it is establishing, promoting, and edifying entities *that are distinct from itself.* The Church imitates the Lord in this—this is the same thing God did in creating us. All the families of the earth are to be discipled by the Church (Gen. 12:3). All the nations of the earth are to be discipled by the Church (Matt. 28:18–20). And when the process is done, these families and nations have not been absorbed into the Borg. Rather, they have become more like themselves than they ever could have done on their own.

It should not be surprising that after I have urged the establishment of a mere Christendom for some time, questions about the First Amendment might arise. It would appear that I am trespassing on the sacred precincts. It would seem that I am strolling across the manicured lawns of the Temple grounds, in order to have a better shot at kicking one of the sacred geese.

So perhaps I had better explain. My position on this can be summarized nicely and in brief compass. It is not the case that a mere Christendom would violate anything in the First Amendment, and the second point would be that, even if it did, we need Christ more than we need Madison.

But, on this point at least, we may certainly have both. The First Amendment, rightly understood, does not prohibit a civil acknowledgment of the Lordship of Jesus. It prohibits the establishment of a particular denomination of Christians at the federal level as the national church. It does not in any way prohibit, to take an example at random, the erecting of a Christmas creche on the steps of the Mugwump County Courthouse. Here's what the amendment says:

> Congress shall make no law respecting an establishment of religion, or prohibiting the free exercise thereof; or abridging the freedom of speech, or of the press; or the right of the people peaceably to assemble, and to petition the Government for a redress of grievances.

Our concerns for the present have to do with the establishment clause and the free exercise clause. We may discuss what lawyers have done to mangle the rest of it some other time perhaps.

If you would be so kind, please note the first word of the First Amendment, which is *Congress*. Congress is the only entity that can violate the establishment and free exercise clauses of the First Amendment, and they can do so in two ways. The first would be if they were to pass legislation that created the Church of the United States, as England has a Church of England and Denmark the Church of Denmark. The Founders did not do this because they objected to national churches, but rather because they objected to the idea that the United States was a singular nation. We were, rather, a confederation of nations, meaning that any established religions needed to exist at the appropriate level, which was *not* the federal level.

At that time, federal government and national government were not interchangeable synonyms. If you take the trouble to read *The Federalist Papers*, a collection of newspaper articles urging ratification of the Constitution, you will discover one of their points to be the fact that those urging ratification disavowed the idea that the Constitution was in any way creating a nation. And this is why, incidentally, Lincoln's phrase in the Gettysburg Address—"four score and seven years ago, *our fathers brought forth on this continent a new nation*"—was such a masterpiece of revisionist history.

In fact, this original understanding of the First Amendment provides us with a model of mere Christendom. The principle of organization between different Christian states need not take a stand on the denominational questions that divide the states from one another. That is what I am arguing for. This is the pattern for mere Christendom. But this cannot be done, let it be said in passing, if Michigan were under Islamic sharia law and South Dakota under Lutheranism. Religiousdom does not provide a principle of unity at all.

Christ does.

CHAPTER 9

All Liberty Is Founded
in Christ

We have already seen that Christ is the foundation of every true form of liberty. Civic liberty is an impossibility for a people who are enslaved to their lusts. For such a people, constitutional liberties are nothing but paper liberties—the kind of thin surety that tends to satisfy slaves who need to be flattered by their masters. My argument is not just that mere Christendom is consistent with true forms of personal liberty. The argument is that some sort of mere Christendom is the only place where it is possible to gain and maintain true liberty. It is the foundation upon which liberty must be built.

Here is Samuel Adams on the subject: "Neither the wisest constitution nor the wisest laws will secure the liberty and happiness of a people whose manners are universally corrupt."[1]

His cousin John Adams said that our Constitution presupposes a moral and a religious people. It is "wholly unfit" for any other.[2]

This is why Jesus is absolutely necessary to any civic reformation worth having. If you want a nation of pot-smoking fornicators to be free, you want something that is not going to happen. Before giving speeches in favor of such a proposition, you might want to consider saving your breath for walking uphill. Republics do not exist without republican virtue. And virtue does not exist apart from the grace of God, as offered in the message of the death and resurrection of Jesus Christ. This is why, if our freedoms are to return, secularism has to go.

So liberty is the work of the Spirit of God, which brings us to another crucial point. The Spirit moves as He wills. He is like the breeze, which cannot be bottled or contained. This is quite true when it comes to evangelism and the growth of the Church, but it remains true when we trace the work of the Spirit through the Church in bringing about civic liberty.

At different times in history, the Spirit anoints different men, different movements, different civic currents, different

1. William V. Wells, *The Life and Public Services of Samuel Adams* (Boston: Little, Brown, and Company, 1865), 22.
2. "From John Adams to Massachusetts Militia, 11 October 1798," Founders Online, National Archives, https://founders.archives.gov/documents/Adams/99-02-02-3102.

nations, making them the delivery platform of His glorious work. If the Spirit then moves on, the besotted curators of the Ichabod Museum will still want to lecture us all on the importance of their dead relics. But liberty—and follow me closely here—*liberty itself is free.*

Liberty cannot be locked up in a cage, whether that cage is a party platform, a national constitution, a bill of rights, or a campaign slogan. Liberty exists, or does not exist, in the hearts of the people. If the people are free, then civic freedom for the people becomes a possibility.

One time, when I had waxed eloquent on this theme, a reader from the UK objected to my characterization of the House of Hanover as "tyrannical." Britain was the birthplace of constitutional liberties, and so how was it possible for me to characterize the actions of Parliament as tyrannical?

The answer is that it is easy—the battle for liberty never ceases, and it never ceases anywhere. Tyrants are always waiting in the wings, looking for an opportunity. When the people become complacent, drifting into sloth and lust, they have that opportunity—and they *always* take it. What do you have to do in order to have a garden full of weeds? The answer to this trick question is *nothing*.

A great blow for civic liberty was struck in the establishment of the Magna Carta. Arbitrary taxation was out. That was established as a foundational legal principle in

England. But the battle for liberty ebbs and flows. Liberty does not take off like a rocket ship—there are advances, there are setbacks, there is confusion about the setbacks, there is a revival of learning, there are advances, and the cycle starts over again.

You don't banish arbitrary taxation from the world, and then forget about it. And why? Because kings *like* arbitrary taxation. So the whole mess crept back in again. Royal prerogative courts, like the Star Chamber, came into existence and began to rob the English people of the liberties they were supposed to have, and still did have, on paper anyway.

As part of the long battle for liberty, the English people in the seventeenth century rose up and abolished arbitrary government. But like a burglar who finds one window locked, and who moves on to the next one, those with a despotic turn of mind immediately moved on to another device. They had not all been banished to the moon. They were all still here, and people with power soon wanted more of it. It is "necessary," they say, with a deeply concerned look. "What about the children?"

So in the seventeenth century the battle for liberty was between the Crown and Parliament, and Parliament was in the right. In the eighteenth century, the battle for liberty was between Parliament and the colonies, and the colonies were in the right. No one institution or nation or entity is indefectible. Bad men show up everywhere, and I wouldn't be at all surprised if our final liberties were eventually removed by the Czar of All Fourth of July Celebrations.

☧

In our time, the central threat to our liberties is the administrative state. Among a free people, laws are only binding (i.e., they are only laws) if they are passed and approved by the legislature. The legislature is not authorized to delegate this authority to anyone, and when they attempt to do so, it is dereliction of their solemn responsibility. Someone might plead necessity, and say that administrative law is too extensive and too complex for a legislature to understand, still less to pass. The reply to this is simple—if a set of regulations is too burdensome for the legislature to pass, then it is too burdensome for us to live under.

The next question is therefore a practical one. Say that we have come to our senses and have found that our representatives in Congress have sold us into bondage. What now? There are two aspects of this "what now?" problem. The first has to do with lawfulness. We have to fix it in our minds that the current setup is deeply and profoundly unconstitutional, illegal, unlawful, and immoral. The second has to do with prudence. How may we best resist this massive encroachment?

That may be described as the problem of getting Gideon out of the wine vat and over to the city park where the Baal is.

☧

We live in a generation that is totalitarian in principle, having accepted all the basic totalitarian premises. Denying the

Lordship of Jesus Christ drives you to those premises—for if Jesus is not Lord, then there is a vacancy that men will always want to fill. Without an exhaustive rule through the predestinating love of the Father, unbelieving men will always see a job opening. They will want to fill that gap. They mimic the Father's omnipotence, which is where we get the totalitarian part. They also try to mimic His love, which is how we get the tolerance farce. And so it is that we find ourselves suffocating under this totalitolerance.

Secularism is simply not capable of sustaining limited government. It cannot be done, and this is a problem. Because men are sinners, they require governance. Because men are sinners, they cannot be trusted with governance. Limited government is therefore the first and foundational problem to be solved in any exercise of practical theology.

That said, it is a problem that cannot be solved apart from the widespread dissemination of the gospel among the people.

Incidentally, if you solve the problem of limited government by denying any real need for limited government, this is not an exercise in creative problem-solving, but rather an example of going over to the adversary. The Spirit of God is the spirit of liberty. The Holy Spirit is not the spirit of coercion. The impulse to control everything is the machinery of Isengard, and those who want to be a cog in that machinery have all their aspirations pointed in the wrong direction.

If the gospel runs freely, enough people are converted to enable them to understand the problem. If that happens, enough people are converted to enable them to begin to execute a biblical solution—a sample of which we can see in the form of government our nation had at the founding (checks and balances, separation of powers, etc.). That form of government really was a glorious achievement, and it should be no surprise that it is routinely disparaged by our generation of *soi-disant* political theorists, *a.k.a.* fiddlers and fussers. "You can't put banana peels in *that* can! What are you, evil?"

The gospel, pure and unadulterated, is therefore the thing that Christians must emphasize, and that the adversary will always attack. The adversary will attack it from without by malevolent persecution and from within by disingenuous corruption. If we don't understand the tactics behind the corruption, then when the time comes we will be mystified by the persecution. We will not understand what our persecutors are up to, because we have not understood what our preachers were up to.

I would go further. The loftier the pretensions of the power, the more meddlesome, inhuman and oppressive it will be. Theocracy is the worst of all possible governments. All political power is at best a necessary evil: but it is least evil when its sanctions are most modest and commonplace, when it claims no more than to be useful or convenient and sets itself strictly limited objectives.

> Anything transcendental or spiritual, or even anything
> very strongly ethical, in its pretensions is dangerous,
> and encourages it to meddle with our private lives.[3]

My agreement with part of this, and disagreement with the other part, is why I have in the past called myself a theocratic libertarian. As should be easy to see, my agreement with Lewis is on the "live and let live" end of things. Like Lewis, I want government to be modest and to set for itself strictly limited objectives. Unlike Lewis, I believe that requiring government to be modest in this way is a "strongly ethical" requirement. And as a strong ethical requirement, it requires a transcendental grounding.

When I tell an ordinary citizen that he must not steal, I should be in a position to answer the question if he wonders why. If I tell my government that it must be modest, what do I do in the face of the same question? For—believe me—governments want to misuse their power more than ordinary citizens want to steal. My elected representatives want to steal from me more than my next-door neighbor does. That being the case, they must be told not to—which is a strong ethical requirement. As such, like all ethical requirements, *it requires transcendental grounding*.

The natural assumption that many make is that the higher the claims for governing authority, the higher the aims of actual governance will be. This is the assumption that Lewis

3. C.S. Lewis, "Lilies That Fester," in *C.S. Lewis Essay Collection and Other Short Pieces*, ed. Lesley Walmsley (New York: HarperCollins, 2000), 372.

is making here. In other words, if we grant that God has established the authority at all, then the authority must have a double-0 rating and can do whatever it wants.

But this does not follow. A government appointed by God to be a ministering servant is not a government appointed by God to be a swaggering bully. Divinely established authorities can also be put under severe restrictions—and in Scripture, the authorities have been.

So if we withhold divine sanction from government in order to keep them from claiming too much authority, we discover that we have simply opened the door to allow them to claim *all* authority. If there is no recognized God over the state, then who has now become god? Who is now the highest authority in the lives of those governed? I am far more likely to find myself governed by a swaggering bully who recognizes no authority whatsoever above him than by a swaggering bully who feels he needs to justify his behavior from Scripture. In a dispute with the latter, I at least have something to appeal to.

But the former situation is precisely the position we are currently in. We wrestle not against flesh and blood, but against principalities, powers, and pecksniffs. Lewis worried about "meddlesome" rulers—you know, the kind who would make you sort your garbage into different-colored bins. The kind who would shut down your kid's lemonade stand. The kind who would confiscate half your income. The kind who fine florists for not celebrating vice. *That* kind. The kind we got.

It turns out that overweening conceit in rulers requires a strong theocratic restraint.

☧

If there is a court of appeal past our human government, then in principle I have admitted theocracy. If there is no court of appeal past them, then I have just made *them* god. Having made them god, I discover that I am still in a theocracy, but instead of a loving Father, the *theos* of this system is corrupt and grasping, mendacious and low, and full of a flatulent hubris. Requiring government to remain modest and within the bounds of sanity is therefore one of the most profound ethical requirements that has ever been promulgated among men.

So if you agree with Jefferson, as I do, that that government is best which governs least, then it follows from this that that government is best which appeals to the divine will of Heaven the least. But for what it does do, and with regard to what it forbids itself to do, it must learn to heed *and obey* the most powerful "thou shalt nots" ever uttered.

Whatever appeals there are to Heaven must therefore be the kind of appeals that reinforce the limitations and boundaries on government. One of the central things that this government must learn to appeal to is the fact that Heaven insists that the rulers refrain from overreach and arrogance. This is why I have argued so often, and so forcefully, for the jealous protection of free markets. The issue at stake is *this* issue. Because Jesus is Lord, we proclaim free grace, which results in free men, which results in free markets.

This doctrinal point about the nature of men is one that Lewis himself makes in his essay called "Membership," when he says there are two approaches to democracy. He believed the "false, romantic" view of democracy was that which thinks all men so good "that they deserve a share in the government of the commonwealth, and so wise that the commonwealth needs their advice." This view really is pernicious. "On the other hand, you may believe fallen men to be so wicked that not one of them can be trusted with any irresponsible power over his fellows."[4]

I take a brief moment here to dismiss any form of Christian anarchy. What governmental power exists must be fixed, defined, nailed down, watched very carefully, even though it is swathed in the duct tape of multiple Bible verses about man's depravity. To take government down to zero is simply to create manifold opportunities for *ad hoc* warlords. Theocratic libertarianism suspects the hearts of all men, all the time, while anarchy, eternally suspicious of the current rulers, fails to suspect the hearts of those forming hypothetical militias on the fly.

But some still react to the *word* theocracy in superstitious ways. They are like the ancient Romans who were willing to

4. Lewis, "Membership," in *C.S. Lewis Essay Collection and Other Short Pieces*, 336.

turn over the whole operation to Julius Caesar, but would not permit him the use of the *word* emperor. Or like Americans, who have granted their presidents more authority than many medieval kings would ever dream of, but would flip out over use of the *word* king.

Why are we so afraid of theocracy? What might happen? Might we go on a rampage and kill sixty million babies? Yeah, that would be bad. Better not risk it. Might we set up a surveillance state, with camera clusters pointed in every direction at all the intersections? Right—theocracies are terrible like that.

The real reason why our current rulers want us to react violently whenever we hear the word *theocracy* is that petty gods are always jealous of their position, and dread any talk of a Lord who rose from the dead.

PART THREE

Lies about Mere Christendom

CHAPTER 10

"Christendom Would Be Oppressive"

W henever you propose something, as I propose a return to mere Christendom, one of the natural objections people raise is the objection of trajectories—as in "that's all very well, but what might this lead to next?" Given the sinfulness of this world, and the genius we have for corrupting everything we touch, this is actually a reasonable question.

What is unreasonable, however, is the way the question is asked. It is posed as though the questioner were standing in a neutral zone, a place with no consequences whatsoever. But whenever we choose, there will be consequences to that choice. This applies to *all* the choices. If you stand at a crossroads, it would be wise to consider the consequences of going right. But you must also take into account the consequences of going left and standing still. It would be folly to pretend to yourself that only one of the options had possible ramifications that were negative. If someone opts for that folly, you may be sure that the path that they say we cannot risk will be the path of obedience, doing what God says to do.

When people say that such a Christendom would be "oppressive," one answer would be to ask them to look around at what is going on now. If we are in the fire, and someone suggests getting back in the frying pan, it is hardly to the point to suggest that this might lead to us falling into the fire.

You see, if we accept that Jesus is Lord, and that He is the final authority in our civic and public affairs, we might find ourselves, much to the consternation of fair-minded individuals, burning witches and stoning rebellious teenagers. See? We can't risk it.

Okay. You say that we cannot risk this kind of Christian rejection of secularism, for fear that it might lead to outrages. But what happens if we *stay* with secularism? Well, it is just possible, for example, that we might find ourselves in mandatory celebrations of the kind of sodomite practices that got the attention of the avenging angel of the Lord for the cities of the plain. We might find ourselves dismembering millions of unborn babies. What if something like *that* were to happen?

As Richard Weaver wonderfully put it, ideas have consequences. Moreover, *all* of them do. One of the most destructive ideas out there is that some ideas are privileged in this regard and do not have any consequences at all. You have to worry about excesses of fundamentalist zeal if you give an inch to the Christians, but you never have to worry about the excesses of secularism. I can say that we think that we don't have to worry about such excesses because hardly anybody ever does. And yet, here we are, living in the midst of such pandemoniac excesses. Look at the news, man.

According to the secular catechism we all learned somewhere, violence is primitive, barbaric, superstitious, and intertwined with that other great throwback, religion. And Christians (who profess not to accept that catechism in its entirety) are nonetheless affected by it and are dutifully apologetic for the Crusades.

Evangelical Christians, who do not want to ditch the Virgin Birth or the substitutionary atonement, but who do want to ditch *something* in order to show the secularists around us that we are making *some* progress, will often ditch the idea of religious violence, granting the notion that their fathers in the faith used to take great joy in collecting Philistine foreskins. The principal symptom of such capitulation by evangelical and Reformed thinkers is acceptance of the ideal of a secular state. We need a secular state in order to keep the inherently violent nature of religion from bursting forth upon us again. These are the gods that brought you out of the land of Egypt, and after generations of this kind of thing in our approved schools, it turns out that everybody knows what everybody knows.

This is why, if someone suggests bringing an explicitly religious concern into public policy discussion, the vigor with which he is shouted down exhibits the kind of negative enthusiasm you might reserve for the advocate of releasing 10,000 plague-carrying rats into Central Park.

That fundamental religious paradigms are in play can be seen by how we process the ongoing nature of our own continuing violence. The Enlightenment, contrary to some Pollyannas, did not eliminate warfare. The exclusion of religion from the public square did not prevent guillotines from getting set up there. But when *we* go to war, our violence is pristine, surgical, necessary, and scientific. We use drones.

Now my concern here is not whether any contemporary warfare could be justifiable from Christian principles (for I believe that there are occasions when it can be), but rather to point out how we do in fact justify it. We do not appeal to Augustine's just war approach, but rather to our foundational secular myths. In fact, if a general in one of our overseas theaters obliquely referred to a biblical justification for what the troops were doing there, he would be frog-marched back to the Pentagon for the dressing-down of his life. If a chaplain there were to teach the troops from the Bible on the nature of justifiable warfare, and the fact became known, he would find that his next duty station was somewhere near Anchorage, where he could count the days until early retirement.

No human arrangement is absolute. Only God's Word is absolute. So what does this mean?

If someone takes human choices in the marketplace as his absolute, the end result will be a market in which the fundamental commodity will be the souls of men. But if someone takes the law of God as his direction, the end result will be a market in which a man can buy and sell his cabbages or cabinets or cars without getting permission from some functionary at the Department of Hubris.

If someone takes human tradition as absolute, the end result will be a stifling and oppressive regime, and way too many bishops. But if someone takes the law of God for his guide, the end result will be deep respect for the established authorities, including even some of the bishops.

So take it from me—you can't have the fruit without the tree.

If you take God's law as absolute, you will not take it upon yourself to act coercively without warrant from Him. This

will result in an enormous amount of economic liberty. If
you restrict only those transactions that you have biblical
warrant for restricting, then the result will be far more freedom than we currently have. This is why accusations that a
"mere Christendom" would result in "oppression" are so risible. Are you joking me?

In our current system, a contractor on a building site
can't scratch his rear end without talking to the building
inspector about it first. Tell me more about this free society
you are so anxious to preserve. Are we dropping bombs in
the Middle East to protect our right to be groped in a TSA
line? Being lectured on our potential "oppressions" from
today's statists is like being lectured on public hygiene by
Typhoid Mary. I can never make it through even one lecture without fidgeting in my seat. And they never seem to
allow time for Q&A.

Liberty is not the standard. Respect for authority is not the
standard. Both of those things are the fruit, resulting from
faithful acceptance of what God says to do. When a society ignores what God says to do, and the grace in Christ
enabling us to do it, the end result is what we see around
us—the erosion of both our liberties and our traditions. As
Lewis put it so aptly, we laugh at honor and are shocked to
find traitors in our midst. We castrate and bid the geldings to
be fruitful. We remove the organ and demand the function.

Evangelical Christians, who are pretty much stuck with the Bible, are afraid that an appeal to biblical principle in statecraft will lead inexorably to some kind of tyranny or other. This is because they have believed the slanders that nonbelievers have circulated about the God we worship, and about the Bible He has given us. They believe that this God of ours is okay when it comes to sending His Son into our hearts, but that if we let Him get too close to the *real* power centers, the headiness of it all would be too much for Him. He then might tell us to do appalling things we don't want to do. In short, evangelical Christians believe that their own God is a harsh master, and that if we want really valuable civic blessings, like liberty and abundance, we must seek them from another god.

Christians invented the most open and tolerant society in the history of the world. Tolerance, as we have known it historically, is a Christian virtue. As preachers of the gospel spread throughout a society, and new life comes to more and more of the population, the preconditions for an open society are being established. The more the law of God is written on hearts and minds, which is what happens under the new covenant, the less necessary it is to have standards of public decency urged upon us from billboards. There were all sorts of things that, prior to the last several generations of general deterioration, "went without saying." Once that consensus is gone, you have to start calling the cops for more and more situations, and freedom starts to erode.

�֏

Now some might say in protest that they are quite certain that if evangelical Christians had their way, there would be no more acts of simulated (or real) copulation on parade floats in San Francisco, which is quite true. The observer would go on to point out that such open behavior would not fly in the totalitarian hellhole that we call North Korea, and QED. But they fail to note that such frank displays of deranged yearnings would not have flown in 1958 America, which was a truly open and free society. All freedom necessitates restraint and, for those who have been following this, the question has to do with who is restrained, and how.

An important part of the how concerns not the identity of those restrained but their position in that society. This will have to be discussed further in its place, but are those being restrained at the center of that society, or are they outliers? Is the standard enforced with fines ten times a day, or twice every ten years?

Free societies can only function when the authority of restraint is found in the old-fashioned virtues of self-restraint and self-control. Free governments presuppose self-government. This is why John Adams said that our Constitution presupposes a moral and religious people—it is, he said, "wholly unfit for any other." And it *is* wholly unfit for any other.

✖

All this said, it remains an ineradicable part of the historical record that free societies arose and grew out of Christian societies. I am arguing that there is a connection, and that this is not mere coincidence. I am arguing for a return to the preconditions of civic freedom and am not arguing for an abandonment of them. Unbelief does not generate free societies. Out of all the explicitly atheistic societies that formed over the course of the last century, how many of them were open and free societies? Ah . . .

Religious liberty is itself a religious value.

Religions differ. They differ wildly. They differ fundamentally. Some religions value liberty for practitioners of other religions, and some religions don't value liberty for practitioners of other religions. Some religions respect the authority of the individual to choose his own religion, and other religions don't allow for conversions at all. If you want the fruit called religious liberty, you have to want the tree that this kind of fruit grows on.

This means that if we want maximum liberty for people who don't believe in Jesus, then we will have to . . . believe in Jesus. If there is no God, and if Christ did not come back from the dead, then the bipedal carbon unit that doesn't believe in Jesus is nothing more than 200 pounds of protoplasm with an average temperature of 98.6, and endowed by blind evolutionary processes with nothing in particular to speak of. Rights? In order to be rights at all, human rights have to be grounded in a reality that is completely out of the reach of our elected and appointed officials. And *that* means religion. For the best results, it needs to be the true religion. False ones let you down.

Religion makes people fly planes into skyscrapers. Religion makes people baptize babies. Religion makes people go door to door in order to offer little pieces of paper to other people. Religion makes widows be burned alive on the pyre of their deceased husbands. Religion makes other widows mail pitiful little checks to Joel Osteen. Religion makes people build hospitals in the jungles of the Congo. Talking about what "religion" does in the world is like defining "medicine" as "pills in bottles." I am not sure you should take that. My aunt took a pill from a bottle once and was sick for a week.

In response to this dilemma, we are often offered "secularism" as a low-fat alternative religion. Secularism is an arrangement whereby we adjust to the realities of our cosmopolitan world, and the genius of secularism is that it accommodates *everybody*. Well, actually they don't accommodate everybody—but they *do* accommodate everybody who is willing to be accommodated! And it must be said that the accommodations have gotten much more tight in recent weeks. We can hardly turn around anymore.

First, notice that to make "secularism" the approved religion is to establish a religion. The religion you have established has no candles, altars, or pulpits, but it remains the reigning worldview, the one that reserves to itself the authority to sit in judgment on all other religions. Thus, a secularist magistrate reserves to himself the right to pronounce that Ahmed the Jihadist is not a "true Muslim." Good to know, good to know. I didn't know that the State Department was issuing *fatwas* now. Well, it is.

And when the Bible tells me not to love the world, the secularist tells me that I must applaud the lust of the flesh, the lust of the eyes, and the pride of life. In fact, when the pride of life in a codpiece swanks out in front of us all, I am now required to applaud like a North Korean at a missile parade. If I don't applaud *the courage! the courage!* I am guilty of hate. And, come to think of it, I am. The fear of the Lord is to hate evil (Prov. 8:13). Unfortunately for me and my verse, a gent named Marcion at the Department of Justice has recently determined that Proverbs is "in the *Old* Testament."

So while secularism claims not to be "a" religion, they do claim to be the arbiter of all religions—the faith of faiths, the religion of religions, the king of ki . . . better not go that far yet. Let's give it a few more months.

Second, please notice that secularism has been radically anemic in its defense of religious liberty. They have wanted to pretend that religious liberty was a value of *theirs*, when in reality religious liberty was a fruit of the Christian religion. As faith in Christ has waned, so also has our understanding of and commitment to religious liberty waned. As secularism has begun to function in terms of its own premises, we can readily see that their tolerance for views other than their own is rice-paper thick.

And third, this is only to be expected. Secularism has no transcendent ground for anything. There are transcendent claims, there are false transcendent claims, and then there are no transcendent claims. Jehovah spoke to Moses on the mountain of God. Muslims claim that Allah gave revelations to the prophet. But secularists issue predestinating directives and decrees from offices with eight-foot drop-down ceilings, waxed linoleum floors, and blaring fluorescent lights. The bureaucrat responsible for ruining your life has been sleeping at his desk for so long that one side of his head is flat. But he does wake up periodically to send you a notification.

Now, one of the basic lessons we should have learned in the interim is this. The leaven works through the loaf slowly. The mustard seed grows slowly. The living water from Ezekiel's temple gets gradually deeper. But when doctrinaire Christians get power, one of their temptations is that they want to impose their whole system, down to the jots and tittles. We *must* refrain from doing this, not because truth is relative, because it isn't, not because truth is a matter of community-perspective and there are multiple communities, for that is incoherent, but we must refrain from doing this because Jesus Christ demands that we refrain. This is what I mean by the *mere* in mere Christendom.

I said above that the fear of Christians mistreating Christians was mostly wrong. It has been, and it will be, regretfully, *sometimes* right. The temptation mentioned in the previous paragraph is not universally resisted. But it ought to be—Christian maturity demands it. But if I grant that it will not be universally resisted, then why do I want to run the risk? The answer is that we are not registering our wishes from some neutral zone. I am wishing for a civilization where, my critics would say, a Baptist might be fined for failing to understand the covenant with Abraham.

Right, but I am not wishing for this civilization from the balconies of Heaven. Rather I am wishing for it in a civilization where Baptists are currently fined for not separating their garbage, fined for having the wrong kind of light bulb, fined for providing a Baptist education to their homeschooled kids, and fined for holding Bible studies in residential neighborhoods that aren't zoned for that. In large part, I want out of this secularist paradise we are in because I think it is high time that we laid off the Baptists.

CHAPTER 11

The Biblical Necessity of Free Speech

I have argued that religious liberty is itself a religious value, and that the religion of secularism is a religion that *does not* share or respect that value. If religious liberty were an app, secularism is not a platform that supports it. They respect our right to speak our minds in the same way that kidnappers respect their victims' attempts to make themselves heard outside the car trunk.

So according to biblical law what is the basis of our basic freedoms? The Declaration says that we are endowed by our

Creator with certain inalienable rights, those being the right to life, liberty, and the pursuit of happiness. This is quite correct, but what are we to say to those who object and say that John Locke is not to be confused with the Creator? We will get to that in just a bit. For our purposes here, we will be focusing on the question of free speech.

There is no such thing as *absolute* free speech. There will always be restrictions on what you can say—I don't care who you are, or where you are. There is no such thing as pure anarchy when it comes to how we speak. This means that we are not being hypocritical by touting ourselves as champions of free speech while at the same time wanting to see porn banned.

In the (now censored) documentary I was in called *Free Speech Apocalypse*, you are treated to the spectacle of activists painting bruises on themselves to portray the anticipated "violence" of my words, while their carrying-on required me to have police protection. I was able to give my lecture, but only because of a cordon of cops.

The Christian framework for society is one that brings form and freedom together and allows both to be maximized in a Spirit-given balancing act. Without the pervasive influence of the gospel in society, freedom will collapse into form only, or form will deteriorate into anarchy only and you will have the free speech equivalent of a failed state.

One of the things I learned from Rushdoony is the idea of the inescapable concept—not whether but which. It is not whether we will impose morality, but rather which morality we will impose. As a confessing Christian, it is my desire to impose a Christian morality. But this is not to say that this would shut down the nonbeliever's right to say anything. No.

My point is that the free speech rights of the average nonbeliever would be far *more* secure in a Christian republic than they currently are in this epistemic fun house of ours. If you want free speech protected, not absolutely, but fairly and generally, in a way consistent with decency and good order, then you should ask the Christians. They know how to do it. Secular pagans don't know how to do it and, moreover, have no desire to do it. *It is not one of their values.*

※

When it comes to the history of ideas, it is relatively simple to show that religious toleration, which includes tolerating verbal expressions of ideas repugnant to you, is an idea that germinated in Christian soil. In Christian history, we see it as early as Lactantius (an early church father who tutored Constantine's kids), and it comes to full bloom in the American Bill of Rights. Letting other people express their errors without fear of reprisal is a distinctively Christian ideal.

☧

Now mark this well. I am not saying that it was an ideal that was perfectly realized from the first moment the problem arose in Christian history, which was when Christianity became the official religion of the Roman Empire. For example, Augustine decided it was copacetic to use the power of the state to whack Donatists on the head, which admittedly needed whacking, but still, it was far better not done. Religious persecution had been standard operating procedure throughout the ancient world, and it took some time for the yeast of this Christian ideal to work its way through the entire loaf. But it did do so, and the loaf *did* rise.

> Let her [Truth] and Falsehood grapple; who ever knew Truth put to the worse in a free and open encounter? Her confuting is the best and surest suppressing.
> —John Milton, *Areopagitica*

> Give me the liberty to know, to utter, and to argue freely according to conscience, above all liberties.
> —John Milton, *Areopagitica*

In 1689, after James II was forced out in the Bloodless Revolution, and William and Mary installed, a bill of rights guaranteed "freedom of speech in Parliament." This development happened in an atmosphere that was decidedly Christian.

And the First Amendment was also adopted in the midst of Christian consensus. Yes, there were a handful of Deists at the American founding, but the environment was overwhelmingly Christian. And this amendment to the U.S. Constitution guarantees four basic freedoms—the freedom of religion, speech, press, and assembly, unless of course there is a pandemic that virtually everyone survives. Then all bets are off, and the government can pretty much start restricting things as the fit takes them.

Just kidding. That pandemic stuff was not anticipated by the Founders. Neither would they have anticipated our craven acceptance of the most cockamamie reasons for surrendering our freedoms. "You see, the reason we cannot allow you to publish editorials that are critical of our august leaders in Congress is that we are afraid your views might lead to a drastic increase in sickle cell anemia in our African American communities. Which is why your impudent request to *publish* those editorials has to be seen as profoundly racist."

But the reason it cannot be *racist*, to borrow a page from Titania McGrath, is that I identify as a white person of color. And I say such things in order to demonstrate that I am still exercising my freedom of speech, and they haven't tracked me down yet. Neither have they cracked me down yet.

I intend to continue speaking and writing as a free man *because I am a Christian.* This is one of the great legacy items of Christendom. Why should we surrender it?

☧

Here is a brief historical timeline for you to keep in mind: Christian world > post-Christian world > anti-Christian world.

In the post-Christian secular world, free speech was not the fruit of the standard, but it became (idolatrously) part of their standard. But when a post-Christian secular world has been around for a while, as ours has been, it becomes an anti-Christian secular world. And in this anti-Christian secular world, free speech is no longer the end but rather comes to an end. It is not a desired but unattainable ideal. Rather, it is no longer desired at all.

The reason why the post-Christian secularists could applaud free speech and the anti-Christian secularists cannot is the same reason why the prodigal son could buy free beer for all the ladies. *He was using his father's money.*

Post-Christian secularists were using Christian capital. As the saying goes, the post-Christian secularists were born on third and thought they had hit a triple. Christians invented the idea of religious toleration and free speech, and when the swanky thought leaders of the Enlightenment kicked away all that transcendental grounding, they thought (for a time) that it was "self-evident" that free speech was important.

A classic example of this post-Christian commitment is illustrated well with Voltaire's famous comment: "Monsieur l'abbé, I detest what you write, but I would give my life to make it possible for you to continue to write." But today the downstream heirs of Voltaire are urging us to remember that they detest what we write, and hope that we come to a better frame of mind by the time we have graduated from the Sunny Uplands Reeducation Camp. And they would cheerfully send us off to the camps after they have pulled down a statue of Voltaire, yet another dead white guy.

Hold! Stay your hand! Unhook that cable! He was a dead white guy of *color*.

In the classical liberal order, there was an arbitrary desire to hang the rights of man on a great big invisible sky hook. But whenever you bolt this sky hook into the azure blue, it does not much matter how many extra Kantian bolts you use—the thing simply will not stay up there. As Richard Weaver pointed out so astutely in *Ideas Have Consequences*, there can be no true liberty that is not grounded in transcendentals.

It has not ever happened. It cannot happen now. It will never happen in the future. Secular society come to fruition is *the sworn enemy of freedom and liberty*.

If man is not created in the image of God, then he is simply so much protoplasm. And "so much protoplasm," the end result of so many million years of blind evolution, is not possessed of any rights whatever. We are endowed with our rights by a Creator. If no Creator, then no rights. Put another way, Darwin hates you.

Ideas have consequences, and C.S. Lewis was right to tag Rousseau as the father of the totalitarians. The honchos of Big Tech are materialist secularists, and to expect their worldview to generate rights for the average guy is like expecting them to stand in a bucket and then to carry themselves upstairs.

☧

So then. We have seen that consistent secularism cannot justify protecting free speech as a consistent value. It does not flow from their premises. If you begin with autonomous man as the starting point of your reasoning, you cannot get to the freedom of individual men and women as your conclusion. As Samuel Rutherford would have put it, were he only here, "It followeth no way."

We have also seen that the value placed on freedom of speech was a value that was assigned to it in a Christian era. Christians who believed the Bible were the ones who pioneered the idea that those who were in error should be accommodated. That accommodation is not infinitely elastic (it cannot be, and never is), but it was true accommodation, and it was kept in working order so long as Christ and His Word were honored. Get out a map of the world and put an *x* on every country that has a heritage of the kind of freedoms tagged in the First Amendment. When you are done, get a different color of highlighter and put an *x* on every country that has a heritage connected to the Protestant Reformation. You will then notice that you are putting *x*'s on top of *x*'s. *This is not a fluke.*

But a nagging question still remains for some. Were those Christians who developed the idea of free speech being fully scriptural? We can certainly find this commitment in historical theology, but can it be derived from exegetical theology, from biblical theology? And this is particularly a pointed question if we are willing to quote good old Rushdoony. This is because Rushdoony was a man who was willing to whittle his theonomic stick until it had a pointed, jabby end. And then he would walk up to the classical liberal order in order to poke it. He would then want to ask some follow-up questions.

☧

And so here let me say that two things are crucial. The first is that Christians who believe the Bible must acknowledge that the death and resurrection of Jesus transformed our applications of biblical law. That is the first thing. It is crucial. But the second is that our understanding of this will never be advanced by denying the essential *goodness* of the Old Testament law, dead teens and all, slavery and all, stoning for adultery and all.

And so while I may differ with the recons about certain modern applications of biblical law, these are exegetical differences. I do not differ with them about the need to restore the Bible as the quarry from which to obtain the needed stone for our foundations of social order. When it comes to *that* point, I would simply want to say—"Rushdoony, now more than ever." "If the foundations be destroyed, what can the righteous do?" (Ps. 11:3).

What about now? Where did free speech go? As we disciple the nations (Matt. 28:18–20), our weapons for doing so are Word and water, bread and wine. These are the instruments we are to use in order to make the obedience of the nations complete. These are our assigned weapons for the gospel era.

> For though we walk in the flesh, we do not war after the flesh: (For the weapons of our warfare are not carnal, but mighty through God to the pulling down of strong holds;) Casting down imaginations, and every high thing that exalteth itself against the knowledge of God, and bringing into captivity every thought to the obedience of Christ. (2 Cor. 10:3–5)

We can see how the apostle Paul pursued this in his own ministry. "And Paul, *as his manner was*, went in unto them, and three sabbath days *reasoned with them* out of the scriptures" (Acts 17:2, emphasis added).

Reasoning with people who were disobeying the first table of the law? Yes, exactly. "And as he reasoned of righteousness, temperance, and judgment to come, Felix trembled, and answered, Go thy way for this time; when I have a convenient season, I will call for thee" (Acts 24:25).

I could go on and on about the glory of this, but I don't want to wear you all out. So the concluding point is that if the weapons of our warfare are mighty, as Paul says above, and they are mighty enough to *conquer* the nations of men, then it follows that they are mighty enough to sustain the subsequent discipleship. If the power of the gospel can bring the nations to baptism, then the authority of the gospel, taught with authority and not like the scribes, is powerful enough to teach them the way of obedience.

And so what is free speech? It is not a means toward theocratic tyranny. Neither is it a secular end in itself. No. It is gospel fruit, and Jesus is the Lord of it.

So I want to ask you to work with me here on a thorny theological problem, a problem caused by a number of factors— those factors including the continuing validity of God's holy law, the totalitarian impulses of our current rulers, the nature of the difference between the old and new covenants, the inescapable nature of theocracy, and the fact that there is no absolute right to free speech in any society. And the problem is this. Within the framework and limits I have just described, I want to argue for the biblical necessity of a genuine right to free speech. Stay with me.

I do not believe that an abstract principle called "free speech" is in any way our savior. We have no Savior but Jesus. But when Jesus saves us, one of the things He saves us from is

our own misguided efforts to stifle the free expressions of
others. We do not hang on to free speech so that we might
talk about Jesus. We hang on to Jesus so that we might talk
with each other.

We do not adopt freedom of speech so that we might
fumble our way into the truth. No. We are given the truth by
the grace of God, and part of that truth includes how we are
to treat those who have not embraced it yet.

Before we come to address the theological problem, we have
to recognize that our task is the more difficult because we
are currently being abused and manipulated by corrupt politicians and the titans of tech, all of whom despise any kind
of speech that might contradict them or interfere in any way
with their designs. They aren't even pretending anymore and
are quite brazen. They are a cabal of snollygosters.

If you think that their ability to whip themselves up into a
meringue will be exhausted once they are done with Dr. Seuss
and his sneetches, or with statues of Confederate generals—
not to mention Union generals that look to their uneducated
eye like they *might* have been Confederate generals—you are
quite mistaken. They are coming after the Bible, and after
any kind of speech that depends on the Bible.

You ought to be able to see that red laser dot quivering on
the cover of your Bible. After all, your Bible is black, and the
red dot should be quite visible by this point.

In the midst of this, there will be a temptation that therefore presents itself to Christians, which will be the temptation to become reactionary instead of remaining reformational. A reactionary response would shut down *their* ability to speak their piece because turnabout is fair play, right? Sauce for the goose, right?

Wrong. A Christian civil order will grant them liberties that they have no intention of granting to us.

✼

But what I just claimed is not immediately apparent when someone starts reading their Bible seriously. The problem arises when someone reads through the Old Testament and concludes that a commitment to biblical law means we are to bring all the requirements of the old order straight across.

> And thou shalt speak unto the children of Israel, saying, Whosoever curseth his God shall bear his sin. And he that blasphemeth the name of the LORD, he shall surely be put to death, and all the congregation shall certainly stone him: as well the stranger, as he that is born in the land, when he blasphemeth the name of the LORD, shall be put to death. (Lev. 24:15–16)

It should be obvious that in the time of Moses, that particular blasphemer could not appeal to his Jeffersonian right to free expression. And when David slaughtered two-thirds of his Moabite prisoners (2 Sam. 8:1–2), they did not have the recourse of appealing to the Geneva Convention. But what do these righteous laws and such admirable examples mean for us today?

What does it mean for us who say that we want biblical law to serve as a foundation or framework for modern society? On the one hand, it should not mean retaining a basic secular outlook, decorated with a few references to the gods of American civic religion, which are then festooned with a few Bible verses that we got from the Liberty Bell and the speeches of Bill Clinton. No, it doesn't mean that.

But neither does it mean picking up the Mosaic code with a huge grappling hook and plonking it down in the middle of the year of our Lord 2022. There is no need to have the Idaho Code include a provision that prohibits boiling a kid in its mother's milk (Exod. 23:19; 34:26; Deut. 14:21). Or requiring all homes to have a parapet around the roofline (Deut. 22:8). And here's why.

The *principles* embodied in these laws do still apply, but the circumstances they were addressing are no more. And the central circumstance that has been transformative for all human cultures has been the coming of the Christ.

In the meantime, nobody wants to boil a baby goat in its mother's milk anymore, and it remains just to hold a homeowner liable if someone falls from a second-story deck that was not secured with a rail.

✳

There are two basic approaches to law. One is the approach that tries to anticipate every eventuality, and to have a regulation in place to deal with that eventuality when it comes. Coming up with this kind of law system is the bureaucrat's dream job. This is because bureaucracies always aspire to omniscience and are never deterred by how often or how spectacularly they fail.

The other kind of law is the case law system. Old Testament law does not just have odd provisions, like the baby goat and mother's milk law, but it is also an expression of a legal system that should seem very familiar to us. A case law system is based on precedent, and the principles of justice that can be identified in that precedent. There is every expectation that as circumstances change, the decisions that respond to the changes will adapt along with it, while the principles of justice involved are to remain constant. Our common law system is a case law system that goes all the way back to King Alfred, who got it from Deuteronomy. It is foundational to our liberties.

Many modern Christians want to say that we should enforce the second table of the law (the last six of the Ten Commandments, those having to do with our fellow man), but that we should not even think about enforcing the first table (those duties that we have toward God). This is the uneasy truce they have made with secularism.

Other Christians, of a more ardent reconstructionist bent, don't see why we shouldn't apply the blasphemy law from Leviticus 24 straight across. We should stone the blasphemers, and firing squads are certainly permissible, for what are these bullets but very small stones?

And then I come along, urging us to respect the right of free speech for unbelievers, and it seems to some that I am waffling, noodling, and backfilling. "Wilson is just a squish with a tough guy act!"

No. There is a difference between a theocracy that operates with God's direct involvement and a theocracy that has to operate on the basis of God's written law alone. A righteous ruler would start where Jesus commanded us all to start, which is with himself (Matt. 7:1–5). The first lesson that a healthy Christian theocracy would have to learn is to be deeply suspicious of their *own* lofty pretensions. This is not a refusal to apply the words of Christ. It is a basic application of the words of Christ: "They shall put you out of the synagogues: yea, the time cometh, that whosoever killeth you will think that he doeth God service" (John 16:2).

Some might think it is "clear" that we simply must enforce the first table of the law against the likes of Servetus, but we must also remember at the same time that Christendom had been guilty of enforcing the first table against some of the godliest people in their realms. For every miscreant like Servetus who was executed, there have been countless thousands of *saints* who have been executed by that bloody maniac, the state.

And we should never forget that Christ was convicted on a first table offense. This should give us pause, not because it should never be applied, but rather because of how *easy* it is to be misapplied: "Ye have heard the blasphemy: what think ye? And they all condemned him to be guilty of death" (Mark 14:64).

The same thing happened to the first Christian martyr, Stephen. That was a first table offense also. "Then they suborned men, which said, We have heard him speak blasphemous words against Moses, and against God" (Acts 6:11).

Those who want the government to have the right to kill blasphemers are also asking for the government to have the right to kill those who rebuke their blasphemies.

As a Christian who believes that all governments are theocratic in principle, I want our deep suspicions about the depravity of human nature to begin with our *rulers*, and not with their subjects. I am far less concerned about the blasphemy that might come from some impudent and sophomoric atheist with a web page than I am about the blasphemy that might come from the powerful and well-connected, those who have complete and absolute control of those blasphemy laws. This concern of mine is theologically grounded, and it is a first order *theonomic* concern.

This is not a softening of "theocracy," but rather a foundational application of it. Dostoevsky knew what he was about when he had Christ hauled up before the Grand Inquisitor.

Before we get to the details of biblical law, in other words, we must first have the framework of biblical law.

That means embracing the biblical doctrine of the nature of man, which means limited government, separation of powers, checks and balances, and federalism, which in turn means a removal of many of the temptations to bring in the kingdom with a sword.

And yet, the mission given to the Christian Church does require us to eradicate blasphemy. We want the world to be filled with praise, and no longer with cursing and bitterness.

> For from the rising of the sun even unto the going down of the same my name shall be great among the Gentiles; and in every place incense shall be offered unto my name, and a pure offering: for my name shall be great among the heathen, saith the LORD of hosts. (Mal. 1:11)

So how is that mission to be accomplished? *Not through the law:* "For the promise, that he should be the heir of the world, *was not to Abraham, or to his seed, through the law,* but through the righteousness of faith" (Rom. 4:13, emphasis added).

I said above that the coming of Christ was transformative. The message that we are supposed to proclaim to all nations is that man is sinful and God is holy, and that there is there-fore a settled antipathy between them. The chasm between God and man was bridged in the life, death, and resurrection of Jesus Christ, who has thereby made all things new (Rev. 21:5). Christ's followers are therefore commanded to fan out across the globe with the message of salvation, a gospel that commands all to *repent* and *believe*.

The first part of that message (repent) applies to every creature. It even applies to kings and all in authority (1 Tim. 2:1–2). Part of what is entailed in this message is the theo-logical truth that rulers, kings, princes, and presidents share with the rest of us this radical disease of depravity. When those rulers are brought to obedience, one of the first things that will develop from this is *the idea of limited government.* They will no longer consider themselves lords of the earth. They will learn to walk with humility. When the message comes to these kings, their first application will be to repent *themselves*, and not to enforce the repentance of others with a sword: "He hath shewed thee, O man, what is good; and what doth the LORD require of thee, but to do justly, and to love mercy, and to walk humbly with thy God?" (Mic. 6:8).

Walk with humility. And the more power a magistrate has, the more necessary this is. And the more instructed he is, the more the magistrate will know that the power of the gospel is not to be found in carnal weapons. He should do whatever he can to keep his coercive powers *out of the way.*

When Jesus commanded His followers to conquer the world (and that *is* what He told them to do), what instruments were they to use? They were to wait in Jerusalem for the coming of the Spirit, and then what?

> And Jesus came and spake unto them, saying, All power is given unto me in heaven and in earth. Go ye therefore, and teach all nations, baptizing them in the name of the Father, and of the Son, and of the Holy Ghost: Teaching them to observe all things whatsoever I have commanded you: and, lo, I am with you alway, even unto the end of the world. Amen. (Matt. 28:18–20)

Christ gave us our mission *and He gave us our methods.* The world is to be brought to Christ, with all the nations submitting to Him, agreeing to obey Him. That is the mission. The method consisted of Word and water, bread and wine. In this passage from Matthew, just the words and the water are mentioned.

> Now to him that is of power to stablish you according to my gospel, and the preaching of Jesus Christ, according to the revelation of the mystery, which was kept secret since the world began, but now is made manifest, and by the scriptures of the prophets, according to the commandment of the everlasting God, made known to all nations for the obedience of faith: To God only wise, be glory through Jesus Christ for ever. Amen. (Rom. 16:25–27)

Now if all nations are to come to the obedience of faith, this means that the speech of all nations will come to the obedience of faith. Blasphemy will be eradicated. It will be put to death, a sentence that it richly deserves. And how will it die? It will be crucified in the cross of our Lord Jesus Christ.

But how is obedient speech free speech? In fact, it is the only way that our speech can ever be truly free. Obedience to the gospel of God is the only way for sinners to be set free, and this includes their speech. But it has to come through gospel, not law.

The power to do this is resident in the gospel, in the preaching of Jesus Christ, which is to be made known to all nations for the obedience of faith. The nations, all of them, are to be brought to obedience. This would obviously include the obedience of their words. One of the things we are laboring for in the gospel is *obedient* speech. But this is a gospel result that can only be accomplished by gospel means.

The historian Christopher Dawson once said that the Christian Church lives in the light of eternity and can afford to be patient. But in the meantime, I find it interesting that Luke, also a historian, commends the example of Gamaliel to us.

> Then stood there up one in the council, a Pharisee, named Gamaliel, a doctor of the law, had in reputation among all the people, and commanded to put the apos-

tles forth a little space; And said unto them, Ye men of Israel, take heed to yourselves what ye intend to do as touching these men. For before these days rose up Theudas, boasting himself to be somebody; to whom a number of men, about four hundred, joined themselves: who was slain; and all, as many as obeyed him, were scattered, and brought to nought. After this man rose up Judas of Galilee in the days of the taxing, and drew away much people after him: he also perished; and all, even as many as obeyed him, were dispersed. And now I say unto you, Refrain from these men, *and let them alone*: for if this counsel or this work be of men, it will come to nought. (Acts 5:34–38, emphasis added)

Truth is quite sturdy and has nothing to fear.

CHAPTER 12

Restrain the Worst Blasphemer First

W e are not done with the fascinating topic of biblical law and free speech. One of the reasons why the question of free speech in a hypothetical Christian republic is such an interesting topic is because it brings together all kinds of issues, and presents them to us in a sizzling pan, a sort of corned beef hash with eggs and onions and exotic sauces all mixed up together and piping hot. Some of the taste sensations you might not have anticipated as going well together before you first tried it, but they *do* go together.

☧

I am talking about issues like God's law in the covenant of grace, the relationship of Old Testament law to modern society, the differences between sins and crimes, the central theopolitical genius move of Christianity, the actual charge given to us in the Great Commission, and more.

But here is the bottom-line issue. Can someone committed to the long-term mission of the Christian church, which is in fact to disciple all the nations of men (Matt. 28:19–20), with the end result of that process being the *obedience* of all those same nations, be genuinely committed to a robust doctrine of free speech? The answer to that question is *yes*, with no shucking or jiving. Another way of saying this is that theocratic libertarianism is not an oxymoron.

Given that the topic is so challenging, I made the prose here extra scintillating, which comes from the Latin word for sparkly, and I did this by not stinting when it came to inserting extra adjectival joy.

I believe that when a Christian theocratic libertarian is challenged with regard to his free speech *bona fides*, the challenge is absolutely a legitimate one. On paper, there can appear to be serious tension between free speech on the one hand and the biblical strictures against blasphemy on the other. So I don't begrudge the questions. In fact, I anticipate them and ask a bunch of them below myself.

But what I do think is funny is when I am asked these questions by anyone who has ever been any part of the woke brigade. We are living in a time of unremitting hostility to free speech, and the people who have declared open war on that free speech are those most likely to be supported by those Christians who are most skittish about any kind of theonomy *redivivus*. So cancel culture is real, and the Christians who are kind of on board with all of that BLM and woke stuff ("Shut up," they explain) are also the ones having Rushdoony nightmares. Our summary dismissal of them is just.

So consider this an interaction with committed believers, who aren't woke at all, but who still wonder how it is possible for a "general equity" theonomist like myself to argue for free speech—and like I said, without shucking or jiving. It is a serious question, deserving a serious answer.

The standards of God's law, being rooted as they are in the character of God Himself, do not change. How could they change? But God's tactics, God's strategies, do change because the world is a field of battle, and battles have a narrative arc. Because of the triumph of Christ on the cross, which was *the* turning point in the long war, one of the central strategic shifts for God's people has occurred in this area. By "this area," I mean the realm of religious liberty, free speech, personal freedoms, all that.

One of the differences between the law under Moses and law of Christ as given to us in the New Testament is this. In the old covenant, unholiness was contagious, and in the new covenant it is the *holiness* that is contagious. Jesus went around touching lepers, and instead of Him being made unclean, they were made clean. And lest we say something trite like "yeah, well, but that was Jesus," we have the same kind of logic applied to believers generally.

In the old covenant, the people of God were not supposed to fraternize with the Canaanites. That was basic. They were supposed to stay clean away. There appears to have been a policy of zero tolerance.

> Neither shalt thou make marriages with them; thy daughter thou shalt not give unto his son, nor his daughter shalt thou take unto thy son. . . . But thus shall ye deal with them; ye shall destroy their altars, and break down their images, and cut down their groves, and burn their graven images with fire. (Deut. 7:3, 5)

The examples of Rahab or Ruth marrying into Israel were not violations of such restrictions, because they were examples of complete conversion: "Your God will be my God" (Ruth 1:16, GW).

But in the new covenant, we find a striking reversal of attitude. We are given clear permission to fraternize with pagans: "If any of them that believe not bid you to a feast, and ye be disposed to go; whatsoever is set before you, eat, asking no question for conscience sake" (1 Cor. 10:27).

And don't worry about where the central dish came from. The pagan who invited you to dinner got that roast somewhere, and you shouldn't care that much about it. If it stumbles a weaker brother in the faith, you should care about *that*, but you shouldn't care about the meat. The meat is not demon-possessed. You shouldn't mind sitting down at a table with rank unbelievers. The earth is the Lord's, and the fullness of it.

The membership of the Church is to be kept holy, and that holiness is to be enforced through church discipline. But that discipline is emphatically *not* concerned with simple fraternization with idolaters—rather, the concern is any overt immorality committed by someone who was a member of the covenant people of God, a professing Christian.

> I wrote unto you in an epistle not to company with fornicators: Yet not altogether with the fornicators of this world, or with the covetous, or extortioners, or with idolaters; for then must ye needs go out of the world. But now I have written unto you not to keep company, if any man that is called a brother be a fornicator, or covetous, or an idolater, or a railer, or a

drunkard, or an extortioner; with such an one no not
to eat. (1 Cor. 5:9–11)

Notice that Paul is here assuming that faithful believers
are going to be in company with (associate with, mix with,
hang out with, share meals with) what? People who are fornicators, covetous, extortioners, and, straight to the point of
this chapter, *idolaters.*

Please note this. Christians were given explicit and free
permission to keep company with idolaters who would worship Aphrodite by fornicating with prostitutes at her temple.
But is that not a blasphemous activity? Yes, it is, and *this is
the Pauline strategy for attacking it.*

The mission assigned to the Church in the Great Commission is the eradication of idolatry in the entire world.

So this is not happening because we are now instructed to
make our peace with such idolatry—far from it. Our mission remains the same, which is to bring every thought cap-
tive. *The mission assigned to the Church in the Great Commission is the eradication of idolatry in the entire world.* It is quite
a sinful world, and it is a huge mission. Idolatry is still the
great enemy, along with the attendant blasphemies, and this
means that idolatry must go.

But how? This next passage was quoted in the last chapter also.

"For though we walk in the flesh, we do not war after the flesh: (For the weapons of our warfare are not carnal, but mighty through God to the pulling down of strong holds;) Casting down imaginations, and every high thing that exalteth itself against the knowledge of God, and bringing into captivity every thought to the obedience of Christ" (2 Cor. 10:3–5).

Paul tells us here that the artillery of the new covenant is more powerful than what the people of God had in their possession in the old covenant. These weapons of ours are not carnal, Paul says, but rather *mighty*. Because they are mighty, they are able to accomplish their assigned purpose.

Some people think that in the transition from the old covenant to the new, blasphemy went from outlawed to somehow acceptable. It actually went from outlawed to doomed.

So none of this is written because we as post-Enlightenment Christians are supposed to feel a little bit sheepish about all the Mosaic hardball.

When Elijah executed the priests of Baal down by the brook Kishon, what he did was not a violation of the modern spirit of ecumenism. What he did was holy, righteous, and good. When Moses commanded a man to be executed for picking up sticks on the Sabbath, that too was holy, righteous, and good. And when the son of Shelomith blasphemed the name of the Lord in the camp and was executed at the word of a holy God, his execution was holy, righteous, and good. There was nothing wrong with any of that.

> And the son of an Israelitish woman, whose father was an Egyptian, went out among the children of Israel: and this son of the Israelitish woman and a man of Israel strove together in the camp; And the Israelitish woman's son blasphemed the name of the LORD, and cursed. And they brought him unto Moses: (and his mother's name was Shelomith, the daughter of Dibri, of the tribe of Dan:) And they put him in ward, that the mind of the LORD might be shewed them. And the LORD spake unto Moses, saying, Bring forth him that hath cursed without the camp; and let all that heard him lay their hands upon his head, and let all the congregation stone him. And thou shalt speak unto the children of Israel, saying, Whosoever curseth his God shall bear his sin. And he that blasphemeth the name of the LORD, he shall surely be put to death, and all the congregation shall certainly stone him: as well the stranger, as he that is born in the land, when he blasphemeth the name of the LORD, shall be put to death. (Lev. 24:10–16)

But if his execution was holy, righteous, and good, inquiring minds want to know something. Why is that not to be the law for any future Christian republic you might want to develop the blueprints for? What will we do with the sons of Shelomith *then*?

Thomas Jefferson once said that if someone "neither picks my pocket, nor breaks my leg," then we should leave him entirely alone.[1] As well-catechized Americans, this sits well with us, and it goes down easy, but how on earth can that be harmonized with Leviticus 24?

Sit still, children, and I will tell you. Stop squirming.

This is the hinge upon which all turns.

Many Christians mistakenly interpret the transition to the new covenant as one that acknowledges that the Church is consigned to perpetual marginalization. No, the gift of the Spirit at Pentecost signaled a transition from defense to offense. That first glorious day was a preview of coming attractions.

This conquest is not evolutionary progress. It is not a case of our better angels breaking out of the chrysalis of ignorance and poorly funded public education. No, it is a conquest of our sin and iniquity by means of the proclamation of a crucified Christ.

So I don't believe in free speech because I think that everybody has something valuable to say. No, I believe that all men and women are bad sinners, and it shows up in their speech. The trouble is that as soon as you start talking about regulating their free speech, because it is bad, all the possible

---

1. Thomas Jefferson, *Notes on the State of Virginia* (New York: Penguin Books, 1999), 165.

enforcers and regulators are rock hewn from that same quarry. Censors are sinners too.

When you give the state power to punish a blasphemer, you are giving the state the power to blaspheme *with impunity*.

Keeping in mind the things shown earlier, the Christian Church began its long campaign against the biggest blasphemer—the state. Limited government is the theopolitical genius of Christianity. What I am arguing for is *not* a secular libertarian ideal, where any man can blaspheme if he wants to. Rather, in its long war against blaspheming idols, the Christian Church *started* by attacking the biggest blasphemers, the central blasphemers, the blasphemers with the power of coercion: "And there was given unto him a mouth speaking great things and blasphemies; and power was given unto him to continue forty and two months" (Rev. 13:5).

So here is the baseline argument. Whenever you give the state power to punish a blasphemer, you are in that moment giving the state the power to blaspheme, and limiting a government's power to punish blasphemy is actually limiting a government's power to blaspheme. And the biggest blasphemy culprits in human history have consistently been these so-called lords of the earth—and not the mental patient who got off his meds and is saying erratic things in aisle 7 at Safeway. The state has always been the principal blasphemy threat, in other words.

Pontius Pilate had the power to punish blasphemy. The Sanhedrin had the right to urge him to. And Jesus was in fact convicted on a spurious charge of blasphemy. It was by such means that the greatest blasphemy ever committed in history was in fact committed. *The greatest act of blasphemy our race was ever guilty of was committed in the name of fighting blasphemy.*

"Ye have heard the blasphemy: what think ye? And they all condemned him to be guilty of death" (Mark 14:64).

This fact alone should make every true Christian more than a tad nervous about "executing the blasphemers." The high priest stated his outrageous charge in front of the Sanhedrin, and it was Dostoevsky's genius that enabled him to see that very same spirit in the Grand Inquisitor.

So you want to shut down blasphemy? Great. Let's start with the biggest ones.

Whenever you give the state plenipotentiary powers to crack down on x, y, and z, what you are actually doing—please remember this—is giving them plenipotentiary powers to commit x, y, and z. This is because sinners don't do well with plenipotentiary powers. The doctrine of sin and total depravity is the cornerstone of a true doctrine of free speech, and hard-headed democratic liberty.

> I believe in political equality. But there are two opposite reasons for being a democrat. You may think all men so good that they deserve a share in the government of the commonwealth, and so wise that the commonwealth needs their advice. That is, in my opinion, the false, ro-

mantic doctrine of democracy. On the other hand, you may believe fallen men to be so wicked that not one of them can be trusted with any irresponsible power over his fellows. That I believe to be the true ground of democracy.[2]

And I see more sin lurking in the repression of speech than I do in the speech itself.

And so the central Christian theopolitical contribution is to frame the constitution in such a way as to take human depravity into account. That means limited government. That is essential.

Why haven't we learned this principle yet? When you pass something like the Patriot Act, with much fanfare, in order to enable patriots to spy on the bad guys, what winds up happening is that the act is used to enable bad guys to spy on patriots. So the license to punish blasphemy is actually the license to blaspheme. And yet . . . Leviticus 24 is still in the Bible. Hold on for just a few more moments.

So Abraham and his seed will in fact inherit the world. *But we will not do it through law.* It is the proclamation of gospel truth that will do it. We inherit the earth, *but not through law.* We conquer idolatrous blasphemy, but not through law: "For the promise, that he should be the heir of the world,

2. C.S. Lewis, *The Weight of Glory* (1949; New York: HarperCollins, 1980), 169.

was not to Abraham, or to his seed, through the law, but through the righteousness of faith" (Rom. 4:13).

This means that the laws will be affected downstream from this inheritance, but the inheritance will not be brought about by means of the law. Rather it will be through the proclamation of the righteousness of faith. This will happen when *scholars* start preaching a hot gospel.

This is the yeast in the loaf. According to the balances of Scripture, it would be far better for a guilty man to get away with his crime than for an innocent man to be punished for something he didn't do. The latter is a far greater travesty. We can see this principle embedded in the standard that requires two or three witnesses to convict someone of a crime. One witness can see a particular crime, and be absolutely sure of what he sees, and yet it would be better to let that particular guilty culprit walk free than to establish a principle that would allow for the conviction of an individual on the basis of one man's testimony alone—because then you are inviting *real* trouble. You have opened the door to outrages. A wicked man could take out his enemy, using the instrument of the courts, which would defile the courts. And when the courts are corrupted and defiled, we are all in trouble.

In a similar spirit, it is better to allow a troubled individual to blaspheme than to give, for the sake of preventing such things, regulatory powers over the definition of blasphemy to the very people *most likely to be tempted* to get into real blasphemy.

That's all very well, somebody is going to say, but what about Leviticus 24? I haven't dealt with that yet, *have* I?

First, the executed man there was not a victim of injustice. He got a just penalty for his crime, and it was right and proper for the Israelites to stone him. No apologies here for Leviticus. God told them directly to execute him. How could it not be just?

The Mosaic law as given to Israel in the wilderness was holiness in a kit. The laws were hard-edged, cut and dried, God was present with them, they had prophets on scene, and God's purpose was to define and defend a holy people called by His name. That law was, pure and simple, rough-cut justice. It was capable of killing blasphemers, which was right and good, but was still not capable of ending blasphemy.

> For *what the law could not do*, in that it was weak through the flesh, God sending his own Son in the likeness of sinful flesh, and for sin, condemned sin in the flesh. (Rom. 8:3, emphasis added)

> For if that first covenant had been faultless, then no place would have been sought for a second. (Heb. 8:7, NKJV)

So what I am arguing for here is a Christocentric theonomy—theonomy as though the Christ had come. It is not a question of whether the law of God is just, but rather a matter of how that standard of justice is to be implemented throughout the world. It will eventually show up in the law, but it will not be implement through the law.

And when it shows up in the law, it will have worked the way yeast works through a loaf of bread. It will not be given to the world in a fearsome revelation at a new Mt. Sinai. It will not be given all at once, with the people instructed to guard every detail of the law with the ferocity of Phineas.

There are three basic reasons why this should be taken as what God *intended* for us to do, and not as an example of idolatrous compromise, pure and simple.

First, the Mosaic code is a case law system, not a top-down system. It is not a legal code that tries to anticipate every eventuality and then make a rule about it. So following Old Testament law is much more about copying the system of law that it contained than it is about reproducing every detail of the law. This is what our common law system does—it is a theonomic reproduction of a system of precedents and principles. That is what a case law system is, and despite some recent setbacks, there has been some good headway made. This is why my ideal Christian republic, set sometime in the future, would not have a law requiring a parapet around the roofs of houses, but would nevertheless hold a home owner liable for damages if a guest fell off a second-story deck that had no rail and broke his arm. You look at a situation, discern the principle, and apply it to a new situation.

Second, the Lord of glory has been made flesh, and through His death, burial, and resurrection, and through the coronation that followed His Ascension, He has made all things new. Like Aslan bringing stone creatures back to life, this new life that originated in His resurrection is inexorable and will spread to the entire world. The earth will be as full of the glory of the Lord as the waters cover the sea. That means the conquest of this Canaan will not end with corrupt kings, disaster, and exile. This Israel will not falter at the end. The power that was dropped into the world as a result of God's gospel intervention was such a great power that it justified the shift in tactics that we see and that I described earlier. But it does not alter the end result that we are aiming for—obedience to every word of Christ—including the things He said about the words of Moses.

Third, because God has more confidence in His gospel than we do, in His wisdom He dropped the yeast of His Word, which included that system of case law into the Greco/Roman loaf. This means that as we teach the nations and tribes to obey every one of the Lord's commands, and to submit to all of His teachings, this would include His teaching that Old Testament Scripture cannot be broken, and that He did not come to abolish the law but rather to fulfill it. But He also taught us, and we are called to remember this also, that this kingdom of His was to spread gradually—as we go out there and make friends with the Canaanites.

These are not dark and mysterious tasks. We have already done this once, and historians call that result Christendom. We learned a lot in that initial rollout, and there are some things we don't want to do again, certainly, but that's all right. We have plenty of time—as Christians we live in the light of eternity, as Dawson put it, and can afford to be patient. And so the world still lies before us, and that world is what we Christians call "a mission field."

So it is time for a Christendom upgrade, a reboot, as it were. I am suggesting that we call it a mere Christendom.

CHAPTER 13

The Lure of Hypocrisy

T he Lord Jesus had a great deal to say about hypocrites, those who professed to love God with their
mouths but whose hearts were far from Him (Matt.
15:8). Scripture never praises hypocrisy, and so why on earth
should we institute a form of government that will create
enormous pressure—for anyone who is socially, or culturally,
or political ambitious—to name the name of Christ for carnal reasons?

This is a genuine worry for many believers. They have
often heard that when Constantine was converted, and then
later when Christianity was made the religion of the empire,
just this kind of pressure was exerted. Many flooded into the
Church because that was the way the tide was now running,
and this brought about a major infusion of insincerity into

the Church. And if there is one thing that most churches don't need, it would be major infusions of insincerity.

How should we respond to this?

One time Martin Luther was responding to an objection that said that if we preached free grace the way he was doing, this would result in some people abusing that grace. His response was straight to the point. "Let them," he said.

An argument that would prevent us from doing the right thing in our social, cultural, and political life together because some people would pretend to support it when they didn't really mean it is truly an odd argument.

If we have genuine twenty-dollar bills that can be used to purchase goods and services, then it is certainly going to create the temptation that counterfeiters have to print their own twenty-dollar bills in the basement. But nobody takes this as a good reason to abandon the use of currency.

This is a fallen world, and if we do absolutely anything worthwhile, somebody is going to copy it, pretending that they have done what they have not done. This is true about painting beautiful pictures, being courageous in battle, bringing children up well, running a successful business, and . . . setting a nation to rights in accordance with the Word of God.

There was a great revival going in Jerusalem once, and the people involved were sold out in the love that they were showing one to another. Of course, this created the opportunity for Ananias and Sapphira to try to get a full-price credit for a discounted commitment. This will always happen when we set about to do anything good. Let it.

PART FOUR

How to Restore
Christendom

CHAPTER 14

Two Revolutions

As Os Guinness has ably pointed out, there are two spirits contending with one another in our time. They are the spirits of two revolutions, that of 1776 and that of 1789—the American and French Revolutions respectively. They are not related to one another as B is to A, but rather as A is to not A.

☧

Because the progressive left understands this antithesis better than most conservatives do, they have engaged in a great deal of work seeking to undermine, redefine, explain away, and/or debunk the accomplishments of the American War for Independence. This means there will be no successful establishment of a mere Christendom unless we review the game film, in order to take away certain key lessons from the good run that the American version of a mere Christendom had.

This means comparing the radical difference between the American and French revolutions, and I would like to do so with the aid of Friedrich von Gentz (1764–1832). He was a German writer, thinker, publicist, and man of public affairs. He wrote a short little booklet comparing the two revolutions, and it was published in 1800, the same year Jefferson was elected to the presidency. This year was significant because Washington and Adams had both been Federalists, and with the election of Jefferson, a Republican, it was possible to see the rise of normal "politics" and peaceful transitions of power. America had survived—but what was the *nature* of this thing that had survived?

The booklet was translated for the English-speaking world soon after publication. The translation was done by John Quincy Adams, the son of our second president and a man who was destined to become our sixth president. This meant the essay was presented to the reading public in English long before the translator rose to the presidency, and it provides us with a good glimpse of the early struggle to control the narrative of America's founding. Everyone knew that America was independent now, but what did that *mean* exactly?

We should consider the roles of names first. I would pre-fer to call our revolution the American War for Indepen-dence, but the American "Revolution" resulted in far more than simple independence. It was an event that captured the world's imagination, which meant that many different factions wanted to use it for the advancement of their own projects. Everyone knew that the War for Independence was important. But what *sort* of importance did it have?

As historians, biographers, journalists, and politicians wrote about it, a battle for control of the narrative began, and it began very early on. Some saw it as the first in a series of inevitable revolutions, and so they naturally welcomed the French Revolution as the obvious next step. Others (e.g., Edmund Burke, Friedrich Gentz, or John Quincy Adams) saw the revolutions as strikingly different from those that came after, as different as night and day.

�֍

Modern Christians have gotten used to our "culture wars." This should not be surprising—these culture wars have been with us from the very foundation of our nation. They are not something new that erupted when the first hippies started to disrupt Berkeley. From the very beginning, we have had men like Patrick Henry wanting America to take her place among the nations of Christendom. And also from the very beginning, we have had men like Thomas Paine, who wanted something much more like the French Revolution. For Christians, part of the reason our culture wars are so confusing is because we have neglected the principles that were laid down at our nation's founding.

The fighting that we now call the American War of Independence actually started in 1775, and independence was not openly declared until July of the next year. The war lasted for eight years, until 1783. When the Treaty of Paris was signed, the new nation operated for six years under the Articles of Confederation, after which a consensus arose about the need for a more robust constitution.

So John Quincy Adams wrote the preface to his translation of Gentz's booklet. He makes his basic point very strongly. Gentz did a fine job, he said, because his booklet "rescues that revolution from the disgraceful imputation of having proceeded from the same principles as that of France." Now *disgraceful* is a strong word. He goes on to say that the revolutions of America and France were as different as "right and wrong."[1]

I have already mentioned the issue of names. At the time of the American Revolution, the word *revolution* did not have

1. John Quincy Adams, preface to *The Origins and Principles of the American Revolution Compared with the Principles of the French Revolution* (Philadelphia: Asbury Dickens, 1800), 3–4.

the connotations it came to have after the French Revolution. When we use the word *revolutionary* today, we mean some kind of fire-eater. At this time, the meaning of the word was closer to its cognate word *revolve*. A revolution simply meant that there had been a change in the government, that things had "turned over." An example of this usage would be the Glorious Revolution of 1688 in England. While the basic structures of English society remained what they had been, one king was removed and another one installed.

But starting with the French Revolution, a more sinister and radical meaning took root. A revolution still means a turnover in the government, but now we have the extra connotations that guillotines bring to the situation. When the American Revolution was first undertaken, *revolution* was a reasonable noun to use. But now, in the aftermath of numerous other revolutions, almost all of them nasty, it would perhaps be better to use the alternative name for our war—which is the American War of Independence.

Using the *modern* definition of revolution, it is safe to say that the nineteenth century was the century of revolution—more or less. The first revolution in this sense was the French Revolution, occurring just before the opening of the nineteenth century (1789–1799). The Russian Revolution occurred just after the nineteenth century had ended (1917). During the course of that nineteenth century, there were various street revolts in Europe (e.g., 1848). This century of turmoil did not leave the United States untouched—we did have an event that was roughly comparable to the French Revolution, but that happened in 1861, not 1776. Karl Marx followed our Civil War with great interest and saw in it possibilities for the kind of radicalism that he was fomenting.

But the point I am making here, and which I want to make in the strongest possible way, was that the American War of Independence was *not* the first in this series, but was rather a different kind of event entirely. We took a different path. Edmund Burke, that great and insightful enemy of the wrong kind of revolution, the man who predicted the Terror *before* it happened in France, was an English parliamentarian statesman . . . who took the side of the Americans. The constitutional radicals were in control of Parliament, while the conservatives fighting for the basic principles of the English Constitution were here in America.

Of course, this requires explanation.

When the Stamp Act was passed in 1765, the American reaction was hot. But the problem was not the amount of the tax *per se*, but rather the constitutional authority to tax. What would you do, as a resident of Montana, if one day you received a tax bill authorized by the legislature of Rhode Island? Take a step further. Suppose the bill was only for five dollars, and your friends tried to quiet you down by pointing out that it was *only* five dollars. You would hopefully point out that the amount was not the *point*. The point would be that Rhode Island had no lawful jurisdiction over you. That *would* be the point, right?

Parliament was the legislative body for England. The colonies all had their *own* lawfully constituted legislatures. This is what was meant by the phrase "no taxation without representation." Because the colonists had no representatives in Parliament (but did have representatives in their *own* legislatures), it was therefore completely out of line for Parliament to levy a tax on Virginians, Marylanders, or Pennsylvanians.

But how had Parliament come to think that it *did* have such a right? The answer requires us to go back one more century. In the previous century, the English Civil War had resulted in Charles I being executed in 1649. As a consequence, Oliver Cromwell ruled (not as king but Lord Protector) during a period known as the Interregnum (1649–1660). After Cromwell died, his son Richard did not demonstrate the same competence of his father, and so Charles II was brought back to the throne in the Restoration (1660). He ruled for a bit, and when he died, he left no legitimate heir, which meant his brother, James II, took over.

Unfortunately, James was a Catholic with a bigoted streak. He mismanaged his rule rather badly, and so in 1688, he was evicted from the throne and replaced by William and Mary.

This event was called the Bloodless Revolution, or the Glorious Revolution, whatever suits you. But the central point is that England had not been kind to kings in the seventeenth century. James II was deposed, and Charles I had been decapitated. Naturally enough, after 1688, Parliament assumed, with some justification, that the relationship between themselves and the monarch had been greatly altered. And so it had been altered in *England*. But in the colonies, nothing had changed.

So the problem was that the colonies had all been planted, and their political constitutions fixed and established, prior to all this turmoil in England. They were across the ocean, quietly growing up into a significant power, both economic and political. And their constitutions had been settled under the old system.

Here is Gentz on this crucial detail.

> Most of the colonies were founded before the middle of the seventeenth century; all before the revolution of 1688. The province of Georgia, the most southern of the colonies, and which was originally part of South Carolina, was the only one which received her separate constitution since the beginning of the century; (in 1732) and was likewise the only one for the settlement and cultivation of which the British government had been at any cost.[2]

2. Gentz, *The Origins and Principles of the American Revolution*, 37–38.

☧

The settlements were varied. Maryland, for example, had been a grant to a private individual. Others were royal provinces, which meant that the king was the immediate sovereign over them. Yet others had the authority of the king strictly limited in their charters—as with Massachusetts and Connecticut. According to their founding documents, they had various degrees of relationship to the king, *but not one of them had any relationship to the Parliament whatever.*

Each legislature had authority over its own laws, period, end, stop. The Charter of Maryland, to take one example, said they had the right to "free, full and absolute Power . . . to ordaine, Make, and Enact LAWS of what kind soever, according to their sound discretion." Now the colonists were Englishmen, and this meant they were under the English Constitution. And this meant, in turn, that the power to tax was resident in those legislatures where they, the colonists, were represented. *And only there.*

So with regard to their taxation, English Parliament was an alien body.

> In no single colony, however its constitution, in respect to its dependence upon the crown, was organized, was there a trace of a constitutional and legal authority, vested in the British parliament.[3]

3. Gentz, *The Origins and Principles of the American Revolution*, 39.

The sole basis for Parliament's claim to authority over the colonies was that they *said* they had it. But they didn't.

☧

So the stage was set for conflict. After 1688, the authority of Parliament in England ascended. During that same period of time, the colonies were prospering. The average standard of living for the average American grew past the standard of living for the average European *by 1740*. America had become an economic force to be reckoned with very early on. Parliament had become a political force (over against the king) at the same time. Conflict was inevitable.

Now Parliament's mistake was a natural one. Now that they were in charge of the king, why wouldn't they also be in charge of anything the king had been in charge of? This included all those prosperous, fat, untaxed colonies "over there."

But all the constitutional power shifts had been occurring in *England*, not in America. This meant that when the Americans took their stand, it was on the basis of their rights as *Englishmen*. This is why a conservative like Burke could support them. The Americans were in the right, constitutionally speaking.

Each colony had an executive head, which was the Crown. Each legislature was defined according to its respective charter. Not one of those definitions had any room for Parliament. Parliament was not listed anywhere on the flow chart. Maintaining the point in just this way was a matter of admirable consistency. This is why the Declaration of Independence is a series of complaints against the *king*. They didn't complain against Parliament because they had nothing to do with Parliament.

At the same time, the king had a constitutional responsibility to protect them from all such unconstitutional usurpations of Parliament. And this brings up another point that might seem to be an arcane bit of law, but it is really quite important.

In British feudalism, the king or lord owed his subjects or vassals *protection*. In return, those subjects owed him *allegiance*. That was how feudalism worked. In December of 1775, the British Parliament passed the Prohibitory Act, which stripped the colonies of the king's protection, and determined that they were to be treated as foreign enemies.[4] The king did not step in to protect the colonies from this tyrannical force, and so, in the Declaration, the colonies declared themselves free of any allegiance to the king. They did not have to declare themselves free of any allegiance to Parliament, for they had never had any.

4. John Eidsmoe, *God and Caesar* (Eugene, OR: Wipf and Stock Publishers, 1997), 34.

Compare all this to what happened in France. Take someone from Maryland, who had been born in 1750. Say he died in that same commonwealth in 1805. Such a citizen would have lived his entire life under the same civil authority, in the same civil society. Someone who had been born in France in the same year, and who died in the same year, would have died under a completely new order. The old regime was devastated, while in America independence was the result. The old England was still there. So the American War for Independence was strictly speaking a war of independence—an attempt to recognize the ocean. The French Revolution destroyed the *ancien regime* and sought to replace it with a complete novelty.

The French Revolution (1789–1799) began with a financial crisis. The Estates-General were summoned to deal with it, but things spiraled quickly out of control. The Bastille was stormed, and then the royal court was brought back to Paris from Versailles by force. Louis XVI was beheaded in 1792. The Reign of Terror followed (1793–1794), and some tens of thousands of people were executed. This is the time of the guillotine. But it has to be said again that Burke, *who knew how to read the trajectory of ideas*, set his face against the French Revolution *before* the Terror showed how right he was.

After the fall of the radicals, the revolution was then governed by the Directory, until it was replaced by the Consulate of Napoleon Bonaparte—the dictatorship of a charismatic leader. So when you look at the appalling series of events involved in the French Revolution, and you look at the sober restraint that characterized the American War for Independence, to say that they come from the same stock is really quite an astonishing historical slander.

☧

Both wars had *revolution* in their names. Both occurred within a few years of each other. And unless you were as clear-eyed as Burke, what the French Revolution became was not immediately obvious. And it is true to say that *some* of the intellectual currents that were very popular in France were *present* in America, but not nearly at the same levels. Thomas Paine was the kind of person who could really move things in France, but he was pretty lonely in his radicalism over here. So the revolutionary elements that made the French Revolution so appalling were *present* here, but those sparks here did not come in contact with the same kind of combustible material as they did over there. They did not come into contact with those combustible materials, because those kinds of materials were largely absent here—thanks to the Great Awakening.

Now of course there were some responsible Americans, men like Thomas Jefferson, who were open to the French Revolution initially. Remember that the French had come to our aid in our war. It was the French fleet that had bottled up Cornwallis at Yorktown. And George Washington had been greatly helped by Lafayette, who later on became a participant in the French Revolution.

But even with such historical details, we have to make some distinctions. The French Revolution, once it took off, had its cooler heads along with its incendiary types. Lafayette was one of the former, one of the cooler hands, and in their assembly he was seated with others like himself on the right side of their chamber. In fact, this is where our phrases *right wing* and *left wing* come from—the right wingers were the more conservative revolutionaries. I would argue it is not good to be either, but current events were as complicated back then as they are now.

So with all that said and recognized, clear-headed Americans knew that what they had fought for was not at all like what the French Revolution was seeking to establish. To run them together really is a historical slander and would mean throwing away one of the great achievements of the American founding—a righteous heritage.

The last thing to note in this regard is the fact that the American War for Independence was waged and won by a collection of *Christian* states. When the French Revolution overthrew the previous order, Christianity was included in what was overthrown. That was not at all the case here. Over half the signers of the Declaration of Independence had the equivalent of seminary degrees. The Constitution was drafted in the year of our *Lord* 1789. One of the names for the War in England was the Presbyterian Revolt. A number of the colonies had formal relationships with specific Christian denominations. Over half of the Continental Army under Washington were Presbyterians, and a large part of the remainder were Congregationalists. Observations like this could easily be multiplied.

The fact that it was Christian meant that our republic was part of Christendom. The fact that numerous Christian denominations were involved meant that we provided the beta-testing for a *mere* Christendom.

As time went on, one revolution swallowed the other one. The radical revolution in France, with its centralizing and secular logic, swallowed the American War for Independence in the events that we call the American Civil War. That was the moment when the centralizing humanist logic established its beachhead. But even though the Revolution of 1776 was swallowed then, it has proven difficult to digest. And that is why we still have an ongoing conflict.

CHAPTER 15

American Exceptionalism

We have many good reasons for believing that secularism is on its last legs. If this is correct, then at some point we are going to discover what will rise up to take the place of that secularism. We need to be prepared for such a realignment. But we also need to be prepared to suggest that the realignment take into account the fact that Jesus rose from the dead on the third day after His crucifixion.

And so am I the only one around here tired of hearing about American exceptionalism?

The founding of our nation really was exceptional, because the men who drafted our Constitution knew that American politicians, taking one thing with another, would be every bit as sleazy as the same class of men from any other clime. As

Samuel Johnson once put it, "Politicks . . . are now nothing more than means of rising in the world. With this sole view do men engage in politicks, and their whole conduct proceeds upon it."[1]

Surprise! Crossing the Atlantic did not change human nature. File this under things we should have learned from The Who, who weren't going to get fooled again. Meet the new world, same as the old world—*novus ordo seclorum* needs to come back to Jesus.

The Founders knew we were not exceptional, and they drafted a constitution that did not trust us, not even a little bit. The subtext of the Constitution is not "beware of the English crown," and it is not even "beware of the commies from the Soviet Union." The subtext of the Constitution is that we are constantly to beware of *Boobus americanus* and the inveigling mountebanks they elect. We are particularly to watch their beady little eyes (Art. I, Sec. 2), their greasy palms (Art. III, Sec. 1), their sweaty foreheads (Art. II, Sec. 4), and their glowing promises filled with Uplift and Sunshine (Art. IV, Sec. 4).

That self-awareness really was exceptional. But we have now lost anything resembling such humility, and have replaced it with an Ozymandian pride, and are the laughingstock of the angels crammed into the balcony at the celestial matinee, who have seen ten empires rise and fall, and it is not even lunch yet.

1. James Boswell, *The Life of Samuel Johnson* (London: Jones, 1827), 253.

Those who misuse American exceptionalism try to pretend that they are the only ones in the world who have had these blessings—which means that they will not learn the lessons of history when it comes to the abuse of blessings. Those who recoil from an ordinary and humane patriotism, as is common on the left, try to pretend that there have been no blessings at all—and thus they don't have to worry about stewardship of blessings either. If everything we have was stolen from Indians in order to rape the land, then it doesn't make sense to think of our responsibilities in terms of stewardship.

When it comes to the patterns of history and the temptations of fallen human nature, America is not exceptional at all. Read the story patterns of history—the rise and fall of empires and great nations is one of the oldest stories in the world. Now when it comes to the current roster of the United Nations, I would rather have my grandchildren growing up here than anywhere else. But in growing up here, they have to learn to appreciate what they have been given, and what their responsibilities are in preserving it, so that they have something to pass on to their grandchildren.

Most people only know half of Stephen Decatur's famous toast—"my country, right or wrong." But the whole thing was much more admirable. "My country, may she always be right. But my country, right or wrong." The abbreviated version makes it sound like national interest is the only standard that a full-tilt patriot would ever recognize. The full version recognizes that there is a standard of right and wrong that far transcends national interest.

One of those transcendent standards, incidentally, is what undergirds the necessity of a connected loyalty to other sinners—the second part of the toast.

In a fallen world, such loyalties are obviously not absolute. There are times when high rebellion against Heaven on the part of the other needs to be recognized, and it is time to walk away. But a decent respect for the opinion of mankind should, if this becomes necessary, require that you be able to give an orderly account of why you consider the bond of loyalty to be dissolved. In the meantime, "my country, may she always be right . . ."

In my experience, those who are most ambivalent or cynical about patriotic pieties—flags, fireworks, and fun—are most likely to embrace the second half of Decatur's toast without qualification. They are most likely to support the abuses of statist power when the state is attempting to be some jitney god in the lives of its citizens. But those who wave the flag at the parade, and eat their hot dogs afterwards, are most likely to recognize that the government has gotten itself way out of line.

Take a couple big-E-on-the-eye-chart issues—homosexual marriage and abortion. Take a poll of a thousand people at a Fourth of July parade, where flags are everywhere, and then poll the same number of people who would not dream of attending such a cheesy event. Which group is most likely to support the oppressive tyranny, right or wrong, and which group is most likely, overwhelmingly, to oppose it? Right.

Say that Mom has a drinking problem, and it is time for an intervention. Whom do you want leading and coordinating it? The son who calls every week and sends flowers and a card every Mother's Day, or the son who has been a cynical smart-mouth from high school on? The son who has observed the pieties is *qualified* to say something about the maternal sin and is the most likely to do it right. The other son might actually be the source of the problem and ought not to be put in charge of fixing it.

How is it possible to move from a discussion of well-ordered patriotism and into a question of whether there is a coming crack-up of the United States? It should be possible because that is what we are about to do. It might be emotionally difficult, but it is not a tough logic problem. The duty we have to honor our mothers should not be taken as requiring us to believe that our mothers are immortal.

You cannot build a federal system when the component parts belong to different civilizations. Neither can you do it when the component parts were once part of the same civilization but have been headed in different directions. But I am running ahead.

My commitment to federalism is pretty strong, but nothing in that category outranks the laws of God. So this means that I would want to use federalism to manage the crack-up. Depending on the circumstances, my inclination would be to let them go. There might be times when fighting with a departing state would be morally necessary, but that would have nothing to do with states' rights—the same circumstances would require war with a neighboring sovereign state. If you could go to war with Canada over it, then you could go to war with a departing Massachusetts. If not, then not.

The question of secession goes right to the heart of an incipient idolatry of ours that is found in the word *indivisible*. Only God is indivisible, and all others are pretenders. If the idea of a state going its own way is "unthinkable," then it would perhaps be a good idea to inquire into why it is unthinkable. Only God is indivisible.

Right next door to the question of secession—a right that the Founders should have made more explicit than they did—is the equally challenging matter of expulsion. There needs to be a mechanism for frog-marching somebody to the curb. But enough about California.

A states' rights approach is not the same thing as saying that states know best how to govern themselves. A number of them clearly do not—Illinois springs immediately to mind. States can become tyrannical, and so my questioner asks what would I say about my precious states' rights when a state was being tyrannical on a significant issue like the right to life, and was (in our thought experiment) at odds with the federal government, which on this matter was in the right. Take the example of New York State liberalizing their abortion laws before Roe v. Wade. During that brief time, a state was running ahead of the central government in this wickedness.

Should pro-life Christians abandon their federalism and demand that the federal government intervene and do something? Suppose New York wanted to secede rather than give up their abortion?

Quite apart from the inversion of the Bill of Rights after the Civil War, there can be legitimate, constitutional, and necessary restrictions on what a state can and cannot do. A state cannot set up a monarchical form of government, for example (Art. IV, Sec. 4).

But what happens if they do? I don't believe the federal government should come in to fix it—that would turn the state into a province. I say this despite the fact that the Constitution says the United States shall "guarantee" each state a republican form of government. It says that, but we don't have a mechanism for it, and we plainly need one.

I believe that the Constitution should have a provision that would enable the rest of the country to deal with something like this. That provision should allow (say) the Feds to process things in much the same way that we would impeach a president. The House would indict the culprit state, and the Senate would hear the case. If the state is found guilty, they would have three options. The first would be to accept the judgment and fix the problem—the king of South Dakota would return to being a simple governor again. The second option would be for the state to peacefully secede. The third option would be for the Senate to vote to expel that state from the Union.

Such a process would ensure that something like this could be done in an orderly way. What it would not do is *create* the possibility of "two Americas" developing. That would have already been accomplished by a state adopting a cultural stand at radical variance from many or most of the others. The recent culture war flash points like abortion and homosexual marriage are a case in point.

I can get gumbo and grits more easily in New Orleans than I can in Manchester, New Hampshire. The same goes for hearing live zydeco. These represent variations in a common culture. A farmer with a pickup truck in Wisconsin listens to music all the time that sings about red Georgia clay, and this despite the fact that he has never seen any. This is part of the texture of a common culture, and a big part of what makes it so enjoyable to live in a country as big as ours.

But abortion represents an alien *civilization*. It is ancient Molech worship *redivivus*. The same-sex marriage mirage is the same kind of thing. This is not making the same dish with a slightly different recipe. Neither is this gumbo or goulash. It represents an alien civilization, one with a radically different idea of what it means to be human. How could it not be radically different? Mothers cultivate childlessness, wives are male, and husbands are female. Other than that, everything is the same as it was.

This is not making an omelet with three eggs instead of two. It is making an omelet with three rocks instead of two eggs. And the average diner will not be able to get it down, no matter how many tolerance seminars you make him attend.

The remnants of Christendom and the rising acceptance of the Molech state cannot coexist. One will devour the other. One must give way to the other. The apostles of the aspiring Molech worship know this better than the Christians do. It is a striking fact that the religion of secularism does not have an R2K contingent.

There is a wonderful passage in *The Everlasting Man* where Chesterton compares the decent (but still lost) pagans of Rome and the dark pagans of Carthage. I think it was because the Carthaginians had what Van Til would later call epistemological self-consciousness. They saw their damnation and doubled down.

So bringing it back to the original question, these two civilizations—secularism and Christianity—cannot be cobbled together, however stout the ropes. I believe that self-government in a federal and decentralized republic is the strongest and best form of civil government. But it is a

form of government that has to presuppose a particular kind
of civilization. It grows nowhere else.

Pagan Rome was on its last legs and desperately needed a
principle of unity that the old forms of worship could no longer provide. And so Constantine turned to Christ, in much
the same way that a wino might turn to Christ in order to
"kick this habit." He has one great problem he knows about,
but he has not thought through the implications beyond
that. But once the booze is put away, is Christ then *done*? It
was shortsighted in the extreme to think that Christ would
take the old Roman Empire, shine it up a bit, and then wait
for the Last Trump.

The same kind of situation applies to us. Secular western liberalism is on its last legs. The integrating principle
of coherence is clean gone, and as one wit put it in the languishing days of the British Empire—"everything at sea
except for the fleet." In these disintegrating days, there will
be a temptation to appeal to the Lordship of Christ in order
to prop up the western liberal tradition. And if the appeal is
to Christ, I'll take it, just like I think the wino at the soup
kitchen ought to pray the prayer.

This is why I appreciate men like N.T. Wright and Oliver
O'Donovan so much. We need Jesus in a very public way,
and we need men who will say so. But I also suspect that
with these gentlemen, and with others who are like-minded,

the desire is to "patch" what we have now—instead of radically transforming what we have now. This is particularly evident on issues of sexual egalitarianism, but it comes out in other ways as well. This becomes evident when it is suggested that Christ might overthrow some of the basic practices of our decadent liberalism. No, no, the assumption is that Christ will somehow make it all "work." And that was Constantine's mistake.

CHAPTER 16

Courage and Civil Disobedience

W e are not privileged to imitate the American Founders in one respect. We do not have the option of sailing to a new world and starting over. We cannot move out of this dilapidated house in order to go build a new one. No, it must be a remodel project. The house is run down, and so we must fix it up. Not only so, but we have to do this while the house is also on fire. And at the same time, many of the other residents like it just the way it is and are fighting us tooth and nail. All this means that we need to have a robust theology of resistance.

Of course we should all know that Christians ought not to be scofflaws. We are to be among the best citizens a magistrate ever had—we should be diligent and hard-working, dutiful and responsible, so that we might put to silence the ignorance of foolish men. We should bake the best cakes in Colorado, but not for the homo-fest, sorry.

But wait . . . doesn't the Bible say that we must do whatever they say we must do—cakes, flowers, incense to Caesar, the works? Well, no (Acts 5:29).

> Submit yourselves to every ordinance of man for the Lord's sake: whether it be to the king, as supreme; Or unto governors, as unto them that are sent by him for the punishment of evildoers, and for the praise of them that do well. For so is the will of God, that with well doing ye may put to silence the ignorance of foolish men: As free, and not using your liberty for a cloke of maliciousness, but as the servants of God. Honour all men. Love the brotherhood. Fear God. Honour the king. (1 Peter 2:13–17)

So let's take a look at some of the actions of the man who wrote those words—and not in order to charge him with hypocrisy either.

> And, behold, the angel of the Lord came upon him, and a light shined in the prison: and he smote Peter on the side, and raised him up, saying, Arise up quickly. And his chains fell off from his hands. And the angel said unto him, Gird thyself, and bind on thy sandals. And so he did. And he saith unto him, Cast thy garment about

thee, and follow me. And he went out, and followed
him; and wist not that it was true which was done by
the angel; but thought he saw a vision. When they were
past the first and the second ward, they came unto the
iron gate that leadeth unto the city; which opened to
them of his own accord: and they went out, and passed
on through one street; and forthwith the angel depart-
ed from him. (Acts 12:7–10)

Peter then went over to John Mark's house, left a message,
and disappeared from the book of Acts a wanted man, on
the lam, with his picture in all the post offices.

This was what we might call a jailbreak, and it was not
just a bit of innocent fun. The guards involved were *executed*
for negligence they had not been guilty of (Acts 12:19), and
yet, despite the seriousness of the issues, Peter did not con-
sult with a bunch of modern Christians, who would have
urgently advised that he turn himself in—citing, as they did
so, with tears in their eyes, 1 Peter 2:13–17.

What we desperately need in these times of amoral chaos
is to recognize that the obedience of the Christian man will
frequently be taken by tyrants as something other than the
righteous obedience before God that it actually is.

☦

What did Jehoiada do? He honored the king. What did
Athaliah call it? She called it *treason* (2 Kings 11:14).

While we are not surprised that she would call it that, we are surprised that lots of modern Christian political theory listens to her.

I am reminded of that great line in Errol Flynn's Robin Hood. "Sir, you speak treason!" "Fluently."

☧

So now let's take a quick look at the man who wrote Romans 13.

"In Damascus the governor under Aretas the king kept the city of the Damascenes with a garrison, desirous to apprehend me: And through a window in a basket was I let down by the wall, and escaped his hands" (2 Cor. 11:32–33).

This is what we would call, in modern parlance, evading arrest, and obstruction of justice, and, depending on how close the window was to the nearest gate, running a roadblock. The apostle Paul failed to show them his papers. He neglected to have those papers stamped. He didn't pay the fee. And he did all this in full harmony with what he wrote for us to observe in that famed passage, "Romans 13."

☧

Who honored the royal dignity of King Saul more than David? And who was more uncooperative with Saul's tyrannical designs than David? Had Romans 13 been written at that time, would we say that David honored it?

Let every soul be subject unto the higher powers. For there is no power but of God: the powers that be are ordained of God. Whosoever therefore resisteth the power, resisteth the ordinance of God: and they that resist shall receive to themselves damnation. For rulers are not a terror to good works, but to the evil. Wilt thou then not be afraid of the power? do that which is good, and thou shalt have praise of the same: For he is the minister of God to thee for good. But if thou do that which is evil, be afraid; for he beareth not the sword in vain: for he is the minister of God, a revenger to execute wrath upon him that doeth evil. Wherefore ye must needs be subject, not only for wrath, but also for conscience sake. For for this cause pay ye tribute also: for they are God's ministers, attending continually upon this very thing. Render therefore to all their dues: tribute to whom tribute is due; custom to whom custom; fear to whom fear; honour to whom honour. (Rom. 13:1–7)

There are many things that need to be unpacked from this passage, but let me start with just two of them. That will do for starters.

First, the magistrate here is assumed to be operating to enforce a moral order that is not inverted. You see the same assumption in the passage from 1 Peter—"as unto them that are sent by him for the punishment of evildoers, and for the praise of them that do well." These rulers are not a terror to

good works, but to evil (v. 3). Doing good wins their praise
(v. 3). The magistrate is a minister of God for good (v. 4). He
is an agent of wrath for those who do evil (v. 4). What they
command lines up with the believer's conscience (v. 5). We
pay tribute because they work at doing good constantly (v. 6).

Second, the magistrate is called the servant of God three
times in this passage. He is the minister (*diakonos*) of God (v.
4), and again, the *diakonos* of God (v. 4). The word *diakonos*
is the word for deacon, servant. A few verses later, another
word for servant is used (*leitourgos*).

Now, where do we go in Scripture to find out how to
respond to rulers who reverse all this, who punish the good
and reward the evil, and who insist as a matter of dogma that
there is no authority above them, that they are fully secular,
the servants of no God? Anyone who believes that Romans
13 offers a blank check to tyrants is someone who simply
has not read it carefully and is not comparing Scripture with
Scripture (Isa. 5:20; Ps. 11:3).

There is a vast difference between the dutiful Christian
citizen and the craven Christian who cites passages out of
context in order to justify a continuation of his cowardice.
There is no biblical way to be a friend of true authority without being, simultaneously, *and for the same reasons*, a deadly
foe of tyranny. Never forget that Peter and Paul, the men
who wrote the passages above, were both *executed* by authorities who had abandoned the station assigned to them in
Scripture. And they were executed precisely because they
were a threat to that tyranny.

When we come to understand their words as they understood them, we will be a lot closer to seeing how something like that could have happened. It was not all a big misunderstanding.

It turns out that it really is true—resistance to tyrants actually is submission to God.

✼

Christian patience is all about patience *as we await deliverance*, which means that it knows which direction to look, to long, to pray, and to labor. This means that one of our central tasks as culturally engaged Christians is the task of advancing the blessings of liberty, real liberty—and not the pot-smoking kind: "Now the Lord is that Spirit: and where the Spirit of the Lord is, there is liberty" (2 Cor. 3:17).

A people who are enslaved to their lusts will never be the kind of people who successfully throw off tyrants. We have been offered a series of bribes—free love, porn, drunkenness, government handouts, and other forms of lotus-eating—and these are the bribes that make us content with the dimensions of our prison cell. But a man set free by the gospel will begin to think like a free man, and that will soon enough affect his body, his business, his travel plans, and so on. It is all grounded in obedience, and obedience is not possible apart from the grace of God that is offered to us in the gospel. Efficacious grace is first, and holiness second: "So shall I keep thy law continually for ever and ever. And I will walk at liberty: for I seek thy precepts" (Ps. 119:44–45).

And the verse that is inscribed on the Liberty Bell is this one:

> And ye shall hallow the fiftieth year, and proclaim liberty throughout all the land unto all the inhabitants thereof: it shall be a jubile unto you; and ye shall return every man unto his possession, and ye shall return every man unto his family. (Lev. 25:10)

That is why it is called the Liberty Bell. That is why we as a people used to be free. Jesus used to be with us.

CHAPTER 17

Preaching and Prayer

The central way that Christians are called to transform the world is not to be found in politics. Nor can it be done through the arts. It is not going to happen if we steer Christian students into STEM. All such things are lawful, of course, but the center of our authority is to be found in Word and water, and bread and wine. This is the center of the mystery that will bring about another Christendom and, if need be, another one after that.

There has been an attempt, remarkably successful so far, to build a huge epistemological dike that will keep the ocean of evangelical faith out of our dry little secular lowlands. Now people naturally function the same way with the gospel of Christ as they do with the other things they believe, but the hatred that our lords and princelings have for the Lord complicates things.

Since it is *Christ* we are talking about, and because there are many of our eyes-like-grease elites who "will not have this man rule over us," they have labored to create a construct that will keep Christ far away from anything that matters.

This project of theirs, impossible to achieve when the ocean levels are normal, has been accomplished by dint of ceaseless labor. The secularists have done their part with their unremitting efforts to keep the church/state dike in good repair, and evangelical preachers have done their part by preaching in such a muffled way as to keep the ocean at levels low enough to make this possible.

But if God grants us a reformation in preaching, and if we start planting churches of Word and sacrament *in the power of the Holy Spirit*, then the dike need not be repealed—it will just give way. If the river starts to rise, like it is supposed to, then we may reapply these prescient words from Dylan.

> If it keep on rainin', the levee gonna break,
> If it keep on raining', the levee gonna break.
> Everybody's saying this is a day only the Lord could make.
> —Bob Dylan, "The Levee's Gonna Break"

Unless pastors and elders are willing to read the world, read the story their people are actually in, there is no way to bring the authority of the Bible to bear in the lives of the people. What good is an absolutely infallible book that cannot ever be applied? Application means making a connection between what is happening here in the world and what the Bible is talking about. People want to know—and it is right for them to want to know—whether Jesus allows them to get a divorce under "these conditions."

Now this kind of reasoning is not given any promises of infallibility, but welcome to earth, kid. The straight reading of the Bible isn't given that promise of infallibility either— whether reading, preaching, writing, etc. Nevertheless, the one who speaks should speak as the very oracles of God (1 Peter 4:11) and, not unrelated, not many of you should want to be teachers (James 3:1).

Another issue has to do with informed reason, common grace, natural revelation, and the tradition of Reformed casuistry on such matters—none of which should be lightly set aside. I agree that all of them should be used to inform our minor premise. Scripture supplies the major premise—dishonest weights and measures are an abomination. The minor premise would be that inflation (and related practices) is a form of manipulating such dishonest weights and measures. Our information about that has to come from men whose minds have been steeped in Scripture, but who also have learned what constitutes a valid argument from Aristotle, who have learned how pins are made from Adam Smith, who have realized through natural revelation that the law of supply and demand cannot be repealed by Congress any more than the law of gravity can be, and who have studied the history of theology and economics.

I quite agree that we should not expect every pastor to be up to speed on every last issue—there are only so many hours in the day. But at the same time, effective pastoral care *requires* a man to be an informed generalist. Not to decide is to decide, and not to counsel one way is to counsel another. People come to you with questions like, "Is it lawful for me to join the military?" Or "Is it right for my children to get a vaccine developed decades ago from fetal tissue?" Or "Can I watch R-rated movies?" Or "The employees in my business want to unionize and I am in a position to stop them. May I?" All of these issues, and many more where those came from, require a pastor who is an equipped generalist. He could save himself a lot of work, and just shrug when asked, but that will lead to a certain set of answers, depending on the prevailing winds of the outside culture. He is a pastor and is going to give direction one way or another, no matter what he does. I think it ought to be purposive and informed.

All that said, when I write on economics, I am not just popping off because I am now on the brink of leaving my sixties, and I can feel myself getting crusty and all curmudgeonly. No, I have been studying economics for forty years or so and, if it's myself that says it, I know my onions. Debasing the currency is one of the oldest dishonest and knavish tricks in the book, and the age of computers has simply changed how it is done. Back in the day, brigands and highwaymen would take your purse by waving a cutlass under your nose, and a modern mugger might use a Glock, about which the prophet Isaiah says nothing. This should not leave us scratching our heads about the lawfulness of armed robbery.

I have often argued that Christian parents ought to accept the fact that their job is not to get their children to simply conform to the standard, but rather to get their children to love the standard. If they are failing at this, then they should lower the standard to the point where the whole family can love it together, and then progress together, growing up into a shared love of that standard.

A former student once asked me this: is there not a civil equivalent to this? Is it not the task of the Christian Church to bring the outside world into a love of God's standards for living, and not try to enforce God's standards of law on a surly and unwilling populace? The answer to this is *yes*, but with an important qualification.

In the case of parents, there is a limit to how much they can lower the standard. They have the full authority to do that with "house rules," but they do not have the authority to alter or bend God's black letter standards. They have the authority to dispense with a forty-five-minute time of mandatory family worship every day. They do not have the authority to set aside God's standards on fornication in order to let their teenage son have his girlfriend spend the night in a sleepover.

We are in a similar case. A couple generations ago, when our society acknowledged the general "rightness" of Christian standards, but did not love them, our task at that time was to call our people back to their *love* of righteousness. Our task at that time was not to fight for the retention of Sunday blue laws, for example. But now, when we are dealing with high defiance and rebellion, when the cultural center is being dominated by poofter queens, the case is different. We have to testify faithfully to a rebellious generation, and we have to testify that they are in defiance of the weightier matters of the law. This sin that has us by the throat is not a matter of missing tithes from the spice rack.

But we do this because it is effective evangelism, which is what calls people back to love. We preach the law, and we preach the gospel. When we preach the condemnation of Christ and the love of the Lord, we are doing what the early Christians did. We are calling a nation to repentance, which is the *only* thing that will bring them back to their first love.

We cannot get people back to a love for God by means of sentimentalist kitten hugging. We do it by declaring the wrath to come, and the staggering provision that God has made for ugly and defiant sinners against that day of wrath. While we were yet sinners, Christ died for us.

And this is why I keep going on about the absolute need for regeneration and the cross of Jesus Christ. It is only a work of the Spirit that can give us new hearts. Christian civilization is absolutely necessary, but without those new hearts, Christian standards of civilization are intolerable, as can be easily verified.

☧

There truly are evil men in the world, and this is what imprecatory psalms were made for. This is why we have them. There are men who will grin for the camera over the prospect of beheading Christian children, and our response to them should be to pray the words of God back to Him.

> Break their teeth, O God, in their mouth: break out the great teeth of the young lions, O Lord. (Ps. 58:6)

> Break thou the arm of the wicked and the evil man: seek out his wickedness till thou find none. (Ps. 10:15)

Our psalter has this second example rendered as "O God, come down and break their evil arms." In the face of the kind of evil that is abroad in the world, evangelical Christians need to stop filling up their worship services with sentimentalist treacle and to start worshiping biblically in a very dark world. We are confronted with a great and growing evil, and we are discovering that we do not have the liturgical vocabulary to respond to it appropriately at all. When we sing or pray the psalms, *all* of them, there are two consequences that should be mentioned. One, we are praying in the will of God, and He hears such prayers.

Second, we discover that praying and singing biblically transforms *us*. This really is the need of the hour.

We need to become the kind of people capable of standing against this kind of thing. Read Chesterton's great poem about the battle of Lepanto and plead with God to raise up a fitting leader for our day. "But Don John of Austria is riding to the sea."[1]

---

1. "Lepanto," *The Collected Poems of G.K. Chesterton* (London: Cecil Palmer, 1927), 103.

CHAPTER 18

Nothing New

The unbelieving culture around us shares the characteristics of all unbelieving cultures. And it is a force to be reckoned with. To pretend that we are up against "no culture" would put us in the position of a hapless evangelical football team, playing against an anti-football team. This is so unfair, we complain pitifully—they walked off the field ten minutes ago, and we *still* can't score! That is not where we are. The other team is very much on the field.

We live in an era shaped by the tenets of modernity, and they have successfully changed many things. But they have not been able to change the fact that men are sinners in need of Christ or that Christ crucified is the only possible answer for them. This is why the gospel must always be kept central.

What we are really up against is a despotic culture, an evil culture, a tyrannical culture, a humanistic culture. They have a different god, they have a different law, they have a different police force, and so the Christian response must be to insist that *all of their idols have to be overthrown*. That is what true Christian cultural engagement is. That is the only thing that Christian cultural engagement can ever possibly be.

Disciple the nations, Jesus said. He didn't say to exegete Beyoncé songs in our sermons. But neither did He call upon the Church to pull a "brave, brave, Sir Robin" move. He didn't say copy the nations, and He didn't say run from the nations. *He said disciple the nations.* Not only so, but He didn't say that we could limit discipling the nations to those seasons when it was easy, during those times when the nations wanted to let us do it.

If any human culture is allowed its head for long enough, then it will of necessity become the kind of thing we see happening now. Satan fell, Chesterton said, by the force of gravity.

Cultures apart from Christ cannot avoid decadence. Cultures apart from Christ cannot avoid the abyss. Cultures apart from Christ cannot stand. Cultures apart from Christ cannot contain or hide their hatred of the Father. Cultures apart from Christ must eventually call down the chaos. And here we are.

Christ is the only Savior. Christ really is Lord of Heaven and earth. But our immediate task is not to get the world to confess that. Our first and most pressing task is to get over twenty percent of evangelical and Reformed leadership to confess it. Then we would really be getting somewhere.

☧

Modern Christians in the corrupt West need to make a mental adjustment. Because we are still in a period of transition—from the older Christian order to the newer bedlamite order—two things have to be going on. In the first place, there has to be clear, open, and unapologetic persecutions of Christians. Get used to them.

But the second thing that needs to happen is that our ruling elites who are orchestrating all this have to deny that any of it is happening. They do this for two basic reasons. The first is that they are rank hypocrites, and they still want to pretend that they care deeply for religious liberty. By religious liberty they mean your freedom to think whatever you want about God and man, just so long as it stays completely behind your eyes and mouth, and between your ears. If any of it leaks out, you are guilty of microaggression against, I don't know, someone who suspected your faith might make them frightened. You must be hauled off to the camps so that *they* can feel safe.

The second reason is that they are trying to mess with your head. You're the one who is crazy—you and your paper-cut persecutions. Poor baby lost his heteronormative center!

None of this is new.

> Did not Moses give you the law, and yet none of you keepeth the law? Why go ye about to kill me? The people answered and said, Thou hast a devil: who goeth about to kill thee? (John 7:19–20)

Jesus knew they wanted to kill Him, and He said so. They said in return that He was a demon-possessed. How dare He point out what was self-evidently true?

Solomon tells us that all the human basics are cyclic. They go around and come around again. He is not referring to the invention of gadgets, but he is talking about what makes civilizations tick.

This is why so much of the discussion about "modernity" and "postmodernity" is just pretentious. What we call Enlightenment modernity was just the period when our public authorities fell into unbelief.

Postmodernity is when they discovered that unbelief is a slippery place, and they fell into it deeper.

The guy at the bottom of a collapsed ladder does have some bumps and bruises, and perhaps a broken bone or two, but he also has better things to do than to call his condition post-structuralism.

Our task, therefore, is not to jolly our blinkered intellectuals along by accepting their overblown and overheated rhetoric about how we got here. We have been on a theological bender for a few centuries now, and we are sitting under the florescent lights of the ER in the middle of the night, blinking confusedly, and the attending doctor is having trouble getting anything coherent out of us. The best he can come up with is that we are post-Silver-Saddle-the-one-in-Potlatch.

☧

One of the foundational temptations for us as we consider our forms of social organization is the temptation of thinking that *we* are unique, and that no one has ever been in the soup we are in. Globalization, the Internet, microchips, Frankenfood, and wireless hot-spot coffee shops all make it impossible for us to even conceive of a "mere Christendom." To talk that way, I am told, is to exhibit my delusional side.

But our problem is actually as old as it gets. Our deracinated rootlessness is an off-the-rack K-Mart problem. There is nothing new under the sun, the preacher says, but *especially* not this.

When C.S. Lewis wrote of "men without chests," he did not discover this phenomenon by googling it up on his iPhone. When Yeats wrote that "the center cannot hold," he did not come to this conclusion in a sports bar with fifty television screens going, with the volume turned down on all of them so that we could hear the U2 song that was blaring over the crowd. If he had, it would have been appropriate, but he didn't. Cultural decadence is something that has happened routinely to civilizations for millennia, and it is a sign of our cultural narcissism that we are somehow surprised by it happening to us. The surprise is not sincere; it is not honestly come by. Somebody really ought to read a book.

> In cultural terms, a classical period is a time when all the parts of a community's life seem to hang together, mutually reinforce each other, and make intuitive sense.

> By contrast, a decadent period is marked by dissolution
> of all the most important unities, a sense that whatever
> initial force gave impetus and meaningful form to the
> culture has pretty much spent its power. Decadence is a
> falling off, a falling apart from a previous unity.[1]

Gerontology is the study of how people age, and the people who are hyperventilating over our cultural dissolution really need to be informed that there is a body of work on cultural gerontology that extends over many centuries, and what we are confronting now is nothing new. And this means that what we need to do is exactly what every other culture that has come apart at the seams has needed to do, *and that is to believe in Jesus.*

We dress differently than did the Elizabethans, and we publish books differently than did the ancient Jews. We fly through the air, and the Babylonians didn't. We eat better than did our great-grandfathers. We can go down our roads a lot faster than Julius Caesar could go down his roads. But this does not change the fact that our hollow men are remarkably like the hollow men of old, and that our forgiven men act remarkably like Abraham did.

Jesus did not tell the Church to disciple the nations until the invention of the microchip, and to troubleshoot some sort of accommodation after that. Jesus did not say to preach the gospel to every creature until they start hooking cameras up

---

1. Fred Sanders, *The Deep Things of God* (Wheaton, IL: Crossway, 2010), 109–110.

to the grid in order to televise everything. He did not tell us
to baptize the nations until the rise of the nation/state, that
glorious phrase for some that trumps all obedience, and to
then retreat to the baptism of individuals, if that. Jesus did not
say that all men would be drawn to Him until people with
magenta hair dye and multiple piercings started to get gigs on
reality television shows. Our problem is *not* globalization, for
pity's sake. Our problem is *unbelief*, and it is a very boring and
ancient form of unbelief. We are about as unique as a pint of
salt water a hundred miles off the coast of Hawaii.

Here is an appeal to the hollow men. The reason for that
culture-wide internal ache and the resultant bizarre antics on
the public stage is that you don't know God. And the reason
your sages, philosophers, wise men, statesmen, and late-night
jesters can do nothing to make sense of what is happening,
but flail instead, is that you don't know Jesus Christ and Him
crucified. The reason you point helplessly to the invention of
the latest *whatsit* as the cause of all our troubles is that you
are fighting the Holy Spirit's work of convicting us of sin,
righteousness, and judgment.

You have not acknowledged that the Lord Jesus was crucified in the public square by the *authorities*, and it is far too late
to be hushed up now. A central part of the difficulty in trying
to hide what He did is that He came back from the dead, and
not in a corner somewhere, and then He told His disciples

to be talkative about what happened. That resurrection, and the proclamations of it, cannot be hushed up either. Jesus is therefore the Lord of Heaven and earth, which makes Him Lord over all our cultural corrosions. His Word tells us what to do about them, and it tells us what not to do about them.

So our leaders are not standing at a unique crossroads—this has happened many times before. The decision they need to make is a simple binary one—either to believe in Jesus or not. And the fact that large sections of the Church would be panicked if they did is not an illustration of a high-water mark in theological development. It simply means that the cultural corrosions of unbelief have not left the Church unaffected.

> Christendom has had a series of revolutions and in each one of them Christianity has died. Christianity has died many times and risen again; for it had a God who knew the way out of the grave.[2]

Too many Christians are stuck in the third verse of Longfellow's poem "Christmas Bells" and need to finish the song.

> And in despair I bowed my head:
> "There is no peace on earth," I said,
>   "For hate is strong
>   and mocks the song
> Of peace on earth, good will to men."

---

2. G.K. Chesterton, *The Everlasting Man* (Moscow, ID: Canon Press, 2021), 273.

Far too many of us have lamented with the Psalmist, "I have seen the wicked in great power, and spreading himself like a green bay tree" (Ps. 37:35). And when the foundations are destroyed, what can the righteous do (Ps. 11:3)? Their eyes are fat like grease, and their press secretaries lie like dead flies on a window-sill. And get *away* with it!

But remember: God knows the way out of the grave. And not only does He know the way out of the grave, but it has been His plan and intention to govern all history by this means. He leads us, always, out of the grave. But first it is His glorious intention to bring us *to* that grave, and we must always trust Him as we approach it. He has done this countless times for us. He has done this great thing over and over.

I have written this before and trust that I will have occasion to write it again. The West is dead. Long live the West. And while there are qualifications I could make here—for western civilization is not the same thing as the kingdom of Heaven—I will pass by all such qualifications in serenity and peace. I do this because all the animus that western civ draws from the *ignorati* is because it *reminds* them of the kingdom of Heaven.

Consider the broader context of the "green bay tree" passage.

> Wait on the LORD, and keep his way, and he shall exalt thee to inherit the land: when the wicked are cut off, thou shalt see it. I have seen the wicked in great power, and spreading himself like a green bay tree. Yet he

passed away, and, lo, he was not: yea, I sought him, but he could not be found. (Ps. 37:34–36)

Wait on the Lord. Stop chafing, and start rejoicing. Keep His way, follow His Word. What will He do? He will exalt you to inherit the land. The wicked are going to be cut off, and *you will see it.* Though the wicked currently have their luxuriant leaves, hang on. We have plenty of leaf bags right here, and our gospel pick-up truck is full of rakes.

CHAPTER 19

Inevitability

Many years ago, members of my family were assembling for breakfast, and I believe the demeanor of all of us was somewhat somber, particularly my mother. This inspired my father, seated at the other end of the table, to begin singing an old gospel tune, keeping time with his spoon in the air.

> Cheer up, ye saints of God,
> There's nothing to worry about!
> Remember Jesus loves you, so why not stand up and
>   shout!
> You'll be sorry you worried at all tomorrow morning.

At the time it didn't go over that great, but there is a lesson in it.

As I write about race relations, and sexual lunacies, and petty despotisms, and the abortion carnage, and grand despotisms, and the predations of our ruling pirate class, the impression seems to be that I have gone all Barry McGuire, the way he was before his conversion.

> And you tell me over and over and over again my friend
> Ah, you don't believe we're on the eve of destruction.
> —Barry McGuire, "Eve of Destruction"

So then, allow me to present six stone-cold reasons for confidence and upbeat optimism. Cheer up, ye saints of God . . . !

First, Christians have an eschatological orientation. It is possible for us to know, in the midst of all our challenges and conflicts, that the word of the prophets was given for our encouragement and hope. "And hast made us unto our God kings and priests: *and we shall reign on the earth*" (Rev. 5:10, emphasis added). We were taught to pray that the kingdom would come to earth, not that the kingdom would float off into the sky. Thy will be done, *on earth* as it is in Heaven. Not Thy will be done in Heaven when we get there. The meek shall inherit . . . what?

When the edict of Haman for the destruction of the Jews went out, Mordecai only saw one way out, and that was for the queen to intercede on behalf of her people to the king. But he was a man of faith, and not just a man with a plan. He knew that it was possible for Esther to falter. He knew that she might stumble. And so he said, "For if you keep silent at this time, relief and deliverance will rise for the Jews from another place" (Esther 4:14, ESV). Mordecai knew how to read the story he was in. Scripture presents us with many different kinds of stories, and we are called to discernment as we seek to place ourselves. We are in an Esther story.

Third, centuries ago Augustine wrote his great work *The City of God*. He did this because Rome had been sacked by Bernie supporters, and many Christians who had too glibly equated Rome with the kingdom of God needed some encouragement. The United States of America, as it was in the times of the good Dwight Eisenhower, is not the same thing as the kingdom of God. The disappearance of the former is not the same thing as the disappearance of the latter. The kingdom of God is doing very well. The America I grew up in, not so much. Idolaters are always discouraged when the idol falls, but Christians serve the living God of Heaven.

Fourth, in the long run, stupidity doesn't work. Stupidity never works. If it worked, it wouldn't be stupidity. Lady Thatcher reminded us that socialism doesn't work because sooner or later you run out of other people's money. A lot of the lunacy we see around us has to be subsidized in order to function at all, and the subsidies are starting to run out. We are in that point of the cartoon where Wile E. Coyote is standing ten feet off from the lip of the cliff, holding the Acme Anvil of Deficit Spending, but just an instant before he looks down.

We cannot pray for the purification of the silver, and then despair when we begin to approach the furnace that removes the dross. The Church in America is shot through with corruptions. If we want that corruption removed, then we must also want God's appointed instruments for removing it. When God wants to reveal what cannot be shaken, He does so by shaking. That is where we are right now, and it should be a great encouragement to us. That is, it should be a great encouragement for those whose ministries are not chaff, dross, or loose unmortared stones.

In Luke 19, Jesus tells the story of the ten servants given ten minas each. In this version of the story, He throws in a curious aside—"But his citizens hated him, and sent a message after him, saying, We will not have this man to reign over us" (Luke 19:14). In other words, while the servants had their own gifts, challenges, and fears, they were *also* laboring in an environment that was hostile to the master they were working for. And the point of the story is that Jesus was commending the servants who, in addition to whatever ordinary risk there might be on their investment, had to deal with the surrounding enmity toward them and toward their master. The lesson is that when things get tough, the godly are still expected to turn a profit. When nothing grows up but troubles, we are called to become trouble farmers, and to sell our crop at a tidy profit. And if Jesus said to do it, it must be possible to do.

Can I get an *amen*?

When Jesus rose and ascended, His disciples did not return to the upper room and unpack Christendom from the boxes He had left for them there. As has been pointed out repeatedly, Jesus did not give them a turnkey kingdom. The kingdom of God does not arrive as *coup de main*. The kingdom of God does not arrive like a tsunami. The kingdom of God does not arrive like the 101st Airborne. Jesus said, and He said repeatedly, that the kingdom was a slow-growth affair, working through the loaf like yeast.

And now, two thousand years later, when we see that the Christian faith has grown and expanded throughout the world in just the way He said it would, should this be a cause for *unbelief*?

In retrospect, we can see the milestones we passed in the journey to the first Christendom, and future historians will be able to point to milestones in our era that marked our passage to the resurgent Christendom. But one of our current problems is that we are a convenience store civilization, and we want the next iteration of our civilization to be obtainable the same way we get coffee at the convenience store. We want to plonk our two dollars on the counter and walk out of there with the coffee.

If somebody, a madman with a blog, say, says that if Jesus is the Savior of the world, this might necessitate the world getting saved, he is answered with demands that show us the constituent building blocks of Christendom now. We want to knock on them with our knuckles. We want to squirt the mixed metaphor flavor in from the pump jar and drink the coffee now. We want the world to become Christian the way the devil offered to make it Christian, if only Jesus would bow down and worship him.

But God works a different calculus, and He had His only-begotten Son hanged on a gibbet instead. What was He *doing*? He was making the world Christian, but He was doing it His way and on His timetable. But He *was* making the world Christian (John 12:31). Jesus, by and through His death, cast out the prince of this world. And, by the way, in the original Greek "cast out" does not mean "kept around."

With the vantage of centuries past, we can look back and see that when Ambrose had his famous conflict with Theodosius, this was a great moment in the formation of Christendom. But at the time, I doubt if Ambrose had any idea of what he was doing—except standing faithfully at his post. And in the development of Christendom, we do not just see the Church putting the magistrate in his place. It goes the other way as well. Frederick, Elector of Saxony, protected the gospel when the Church had decided to quit doing that and opted for attacking the gospel instead.

So how is the process of discipling the nations to be accomplished? With centuries, nay, with millennia of bumpity-bumpity.

At the end of the book of Esther, the Jews were enabled by the grace of God to defend themselves, and they wound up killing 75,000 of their enemies (Esther 9:16). Just prior to that, their enemies had been hoping to use the decree of Haman to wipe out the Jews, but at the last minute the tables were turned (Esther 9:1). There was a goodish bit of court politics going on, combined with a little of "no, wait, not that."

> The posts went out, being hastened by the king's commandment, and the decree was given in Shushan the

palace. And the king and Haman sat down to drink; but the city Shushan was perplexed. (Esther 3:15)

Perplexed, sort of like me, scrolling through the Drudge Report. I am regularly amazed that these people are still running what is left of our civilization. Shoot, I am amazed that they all still have drivers' licenses.

I believe that we will be delivered. I believe that we will see a black swan revival. But whether we are delivered or not, it doesn't matter. Faithfulness can be found in apparent defeat as easily as in victory. Deliverance is given to faithful men, and faithful men are those who care about certain things more than deliverance.

If it be so, our God whom we serve is able to deliver us from the burning fiery furnace, and he will deliver us out of thine hand, O king. *But if not*, be it known unto thee, O king, that *we will not serve thy gods*, nor worship the golden image which thou hast set up. (Dan. 3:17–18, emphasis added)

I believe we need to pray and work for deliverance. I believe we need to *expect* deliverance, trusting God for it. But whether or not He grants us that victory, we can at least arrange for a flamboyant defeat.

One of the reasons why Christians are so discouraged by the turn events have taken is that they have not been steeped in the right kind of stories. Smaug is great, but Bard has one arrow left.

Hot Gospel for Heated Times

What we need to do is to bring the good news of the grace of God to those in the grip of our current imbecilities, but I would also ask you to give me a moment to warm to the subject.

What we have been seeing in our American streets over the last few years is an intersectional mash-up. It has been the meeting place where stupidity, envy, hatred, ignorance, and folly have all met up to do a little showing off. They all wanted to do a little flexing for the orc-girls.

The folly has reached the point where it is now throwing bricks and setting fires, and because it has thus drawn this kind of marked attention to itself, we may now make out a number of the more significant contributing factors.

We are talking about the ache of fatherlessness, meeting up with a generation that was drugged instead of educated, meeting up with white guilt and envy, meeting up with black shame and envy, meeting up with suffocating paternalism from the state, meeting up with overweening incompetence from the state, and all conspiring to fill the room with fumes, there to await the death of George Floyd.

And so our situation is comparable to that poor woman in the gospels: "And had suffered many things from many physicians. She had spent all that she had and was no better, but rather grew worse" (Mark 5:26, NKJV)

The more we appeal to our experts, the worse everything gets. The more money we spend, the worse everything gets. And you can count on our politicians to get out there in front of all of this, so that they may insist on the necessary reforms. But never forget that all the things they need to fix are the result of all their *previous* reforms.

> I stood in line
> Down at the County Hall
> I heard a man say,
> "We're gonna build
> Some new apartments for y'all"
> And everybody wanna know
> Yes, they wanna know

Why I'm singing the blues.

—B.B. King, "Why I Sing the Blues"

And the white boy reformer, filled as he is with pure thoughts, grand ideas, and paternalistic pride, is mystified by all of this. And that is because *he* needs Jesus, just like everybody else. Everybody needs saving, and so we really should start with our saviors.

So we are in the grip of our folly. Folly has us by the throat, and no one can breathe. Now a fool can be *saved* from his folly, about which more in a minute, but a fool cannot *evolve* out of his folly. There is only one way out. Nothing will serve but a new man: "Though you grind a fool in a mortar with a pestle along with crushed grain, Yet his foolishness will not depart from him" (Prov. 27:22, NKJV).

God sometimes deals in ironies.

Because He deals in ironies, He will take the message of this small book into some unexpected corners. As the world we once knew is continuing to fall apart, there will come a time when former adversaries—who see this happening—will be brought together in the only way possible, through Christ.

So I know that you are a black activist, and a hard-left radical, and so you have no business reading a book like this. The only reason you are reading it now is because you are obliquely acquainted with some sob sister evangelical, one of those reconciliation-mongers, who shared it with you so that he might score some righteousness points by empathizing together with you, and grieving with you over the fact that there are still people like me out there. That's why *he* gave it to you.

But the reason God arranged for all this is that He wanted you to hear the straight gospel from an admirer of Stonewall Jackson, so that you could repent of your sins, which are many, and trust in Christ, who will forgive them all. This is so that when you die you might go to Heaven and there join with the innumerable multitude as they surround the throne in a praising throng. And there, in that place, God will arrange for you to be shoulder to shoulder with Robert E. Lee. That's why this is all happening. God loves irony.

There are those who would say that someone with my politics can't really have the best interests of his black enemies in view. To which I would say, watch. And they would say someone with my view of the reconciliation industry can't really love the sob sisters. To which I would say, watch.

Let us begin with what that gospel is.

Before naming the sins that must be repented, I want to be clear about the content of the only message that can extricate anyone from any of these sins. Jesus Christ, who was almost certainly a different color from you, died on the cross in accordance with the will of His Father, who is no color at all. Christ died on the cross so that I and numerous others might be given a commission to proclaim it to you, telling you what it means. It means that we are authorized to make you an offer. If you repent of your sins and believe in the one who was stretched out on that gibbet, He will forgive you for every last one of those sins.

God took the sins of all His people, the sins that He hates so much and which unbelieving reformers pretend to hate so much, placed them on the shoulders of His Son, and there poured out His wrath on all of them. This means that when Jesus died, those sins died with Him. This means that anyone can turn to Him and be forgiven. This offer of forgiveness and cleansing is extended to all, without partiality. God forgives white bigots and black rioters.

And He can do this because three days after His crucifixion, God raised Him from the dead, in order to fulfill the promise of Scripture, and to establish Him as the Lord over every tribe. We must believe in His sacrificial death, and accept our justification in His resurrection, and then acknowledge that He, and He alone, is Lord. This means that every black tribe is ruled by a man who is not black, and every white tribe is ruled by a Jew. It is time for everybody to deal with it.

Every sinner must repent, red and yellow, black and white. They must not dare to cast sidelong glances at other sinners, wondering if they are comparatively more righteous. All of us are corrupt enough to be thrown headlong into Hell, and no injustice done.

In the balances of Heaven, there is only the gift of salvation and the wages of damnation. And when the wages of damnation arrive on that great Payday, nobody will be looking over anybody else's shoulder, trying to figure out what *they* got.

The only reason for making any kind of differentiation here is to help those who must repent of the sins that they, not other people, have committed. White men must repent of sins that they have committed and black men must do the same. And the more intersectional you are, the more your repentance needs to be intersectional. And everyone must repent of their lying and their fakery and their hypocrisy and their blame-shifting.

The law of God is like math. It doesn't care about anybody's hurt feelings. It is straight, and hard, and cold, and altogether righteous. But at the same time, when this cold, very cold law is resurrected in the body of Christ back from the darkness of the tomb, it comes to us as burning love. And this is why the message must be cold law and hot gospel.

Knowing that a man is not justified by the works of the law, but by the faith of Jesus Christ, even we have believed in Jesus Christ, that we might be justified by the faith of Christ, and not by the works of the law: for by the works of the law shall no flesh be justified. (Gal. 2:16)

This passage comes in the context of Paul's rebuke of Peter at Antioch. Paul says that we *know* that a man cannot be justified by the works of the law. If we know that, then it is imperative that we act as though we know it. Peter knew that truth, but he had started to wobble in his actions concerning it. We are justified by the faith of Jesus Christ, and not by our own works. There is debate among interpreters as to whether this is referring to "the faith *of* Jesus Christ" (as in, His faith) or "faith in Jesus Christ" (as in, our faith in His obedience). We are not going to go into that because, fortunately, it amounts to the same thing. We are justified by *Christ*, and not by our own labors. We have believed in Jesus so that we might be justified, and not by the works of the law. Justification through our own efforts is nothing but a pious pipe dream.

There are three uses of the law.

God is one, and this means that His Word is unified. But His unified Word can have multiple applications. His law is one, but there are three crucial applications of that one law. In Reformed theology, we are accustomed to speak of the threefold use of the law.

The *first use* is to make us aware of our need for salvation (Rom. 3:20; 4:15; 5:13; 7:7–11; Gal. 3:19–24). In this application, it is impossible to keep. It can only condemn, making us aware of our desperate need for grace.

The *second use* is for the maintenance of civil order. The magistrate can use the guidance of the law as he fulfills his duty of restraining the evil that men do to one another (1 Tim. 1:9).

The *third use* helps the regenerate understand what love looks like in particular situations. In this sense the law is a guide for us in our sanctification (Rom. 13:8–10). It shows us what *love* looks like.

You can see how individuals who are jealous for the purity of the first use of the law would be suspicious of those who make much of the third use. In other words, while there is real legalism out there, we want to make sure that we don't define a legalist as someone who loves Jesus more than we do.

There are some believers who want to think in terms of a law/gospel hermeneutic. Now the word *hermeneutic* has to do with how we interpret a text, like the Scriptures, and so what this means is that they want some passages in the Bible to be "law," condemning us in our sin, and other passages to be "gospel," offering us a gracious way out of bondage to sin. But this won't do.

We couldn't really color-code a special edition of the Bible in law/gospel categories. What is more "law-like" than the Ten Commandments? And how do the Ten Commandments begin? "And God spake all these words, saying, I am the Lord thy God, which have brought thee out of the land of Egypt, *out of the house of bondage*" (Exod. 20:1–2, emphasis added). Sounds pretty gracious. And here is an odd statement about "the law." "The law of the Lord is perfect, *converting the soul*: the testimony of the Lord is sure, making wise the simple" (Ps. 19:7, emphasis added).

And what is more gracious than the gospel of our Lord Jesus?

> Now thanks be unto God, which always causeth us to triumph in Christ, and maketh manifest the savour of his knowledge by us in every place. For we are unto God a sweet savour of Christ, in them that are saved, and in them that perish: To the one *we are the savour of death unto death*; and to the other the savour of life unto life. And who is sufficient for these things? (2 Cor. 2:14–16, emphasis added)

And this gracious gospel is what? To those who are perishing it is the aroma of *death*.

This tells us that the fundamental law/gospel divide is *not* to be found in the text of Scripture. It is found in the difference between regenerate and unregenerate man. For the regenerate, everything from God is sweeter than the honeycomb. All of it is grace. For the unregenerate, the whole thing is the stench of death, including the good news of Christ on the cross. All of it is law and condemnation.

So the issue is objective guilt, not hurt feelings.

When we are held up against the law of God and measured by it, the measurement is always constant. It does not show partiality and does not adjust anything on the basis of how we feel.

It is true that sinners are a tangled mess of spiritual bruises, but that is simply a symptom of the problem. It is not the problem. The objective problem is objective wrath coming down on objective guilt, with the sinner underneath.

Cold law, hot gospel.

When we all stand before the tribunal of God's law, our trial there will be deliberate, careful, meticulous, and altogether just. This is what I mean with the reference to *cold law*. But the sentence? The sentence is *not* cold and clinical.

> Who can stand before his indignation? And who can abide in the fierceness of his anger? His fury is poured

out like fire, and the rocks are thrown down by him.
(Nahum 1:6)

He that believeth on the Son hath everlasting life: and
he that believeth not the Son shall not see life; but the
wrath of God abideth on him. (John 3:36)

So this is just where the gospel comes in. Our evaluation
by the law of God is deliberate and judicious.

But the sentence is a fireball, and yet there is no grounds
for complaint. Every mouth will be stopped before Him.
And here is where the wisdom of God overwhelms all the
pretended wisdom of man.

The reason there can be a hot gospel is because in the cross
of Christ, the hot wrath of God was poured out upon Christ,
and He took it all onto Himself. The word *propitiation* refers
to the fist of the Father, striking the Son, so that you might
be struck down in Him and raised again to life in Him. "And
he is the propitiation for our sins: and not for ours only, but
also for the sins of the whole world" (1 John 2:2).

☧

This is gospel, this is grace. This is forgiveness and cleansing.
This is the foundation of a mere Christendom.